THE MESSENGERS

THE MESSENGERS

*A Concise History of the
United Society for the Propagation of the Gospel*

MARGARET DEWEY

MOWBRAYS
LONDON & OXFORD

Set in 10 pt Press Roman
by Hope Services, Wantage
and printed and bound in Great Britain by
Redwood Burn Limited, Trowbridge & Esher

ISBN 0264 660897 (paperback)
ISBN 0264 663020 (hardback)

First published by A. R. Mowbray & Co. Limited
The Alden Press, Osney Mead, Oxford OX2 0EG

CONTENTS

THE TWENTIETH CENTURY:
'YE ARE WITNESSES'

Introduction

In 1975 the United Society for the Propagation of the Gospel (USPG) is ten years old, but its collective memory goes back 274 years. The family history begins in 1701 with the 'Venerable Society', an ascription of respect applied to the Society for the Propagation of the Gospel in Foreign Parts (SPG) as early as 1706. The other parent, the Universities' Mission to Central Africa (UMCA), and USPG's third constituent body, the Cambridge Mission to Delhi (CMD), were born of that great watershed in modern missionary history, 1857, which saw both Livingstone's appeal for Africa and the Indian Mutiny which led to the British Raj and large-scale SPG involvement in India.

SPG and UMCA were both launched with the formal backing of the Convocation of the Church of England. SPG was a missionary *society* with the very wide purpose of enabling the Church's mission through its own enthusiasm, administrative machinery, experience, and that transferable power we call money. In the beginning there were SPG missionaries, but as soon as there was a bishop on the spot, the Society sent its recruits, as missionaries of *the Church*, to work under him. There are properly speaking no 'USPG missionaries': those on its lists[1] are recruited and often trained by the Society, outfitted, helped with various expenses, prayed for, kept in touch with, helped on their return. But they are paid by and responsible to the diocese which employs them (though this may be made possible by a USPG grant to the diocese).

> USPG *employs* no one except its home staff. It is a travel agency, a roving educational establishment (thirty of its missionaries are called Area Secretaries and cover England

1

and Wales and Northern Ireland), a gadfly, a labour exchange, a fund-raiser, and a trainer of Christians for missionary action here and overseas.[2]

UMCA and CMD were themselves *missions* to particular areas, with their own unique lines in the missionary spectrum. Both had roots in the Tractarian movement. SPG, with no 'Churchmanship' of its own, embraced the theological diversity of the Church it served, though the gravitation of Evangelicals to the Church Missionary Society (CMS) sometimes left SPG looking more 'High Church' than it intended. Today two-thirds of the parishes which support USPG support CMS also.

At a three-day residential joint meeting of the governing bodies of USPG and CMS early in 1973, Dewi Morgan (SPG Editorial Secretary 1951-63) shared the impressions of a missionary from the 'foreign parts' beyond Offa's Dyke upon first attending an SPG Council meeting.

> There was present, almost tangibly, the accumulation of two and a half centuries of specialised prayer and pondering to the one specific purpose of the global propagation of the Gospel. SPG was not an organisation but an organism, with its own memory of every lesson it had ever learned, and those lessons had been spelled out in a host of exotic places. I learned that SPG was always in the course of becoming and never satisfied that it had arrived. It was a process, not an accepted procedure. . . .
>
> That same meeting convinced me that SPG was impregnated with a deep sense of its own unimportance. For SPG, SPG, just did not matter. It was a servant—a *doulos*—of the Church. And I rapidly learned that 'Church' did *not* mean Church of England (something I as a Welshman was readily disposed to accept anyway) but the Church as itself the servant of the King and the Kingdom whose coming Jesus taught us to pray and work for.[3]

Morgan perceived the Society's history as 'a dynamic which operates in today's committees and councils.' Twelve years of committees also revealed

> just how much the thinking of the Church is *group* thinking. Here and there you find the individual genius. But by and large the life of the Church goes forward when people get together to do things, think things, pray

2

things. . . . At SPG I had the quite indescribable privilege of being one of a group. The Society advances by team work.[4]

The Society's work (like that of the Church itself) has from the start had two aspects, always in tension. There is the evangelism to which its jaw-breaking eighteenth-century name refers, a priority to which that name (perhaps providentially all but impossible legally to change) has a way of periodically recalling the Society. Evangelistic zeal has ebbed and flowed in direct ratio with personal devotion to our Lord, variously fed from Non-Juror, Pietist, Evangelical and Tractarian sources. And there is the wider mission of the Church (including socio-cultural tasks) which looms larger in its original Charter, and into contemporary forms of which the Society is continually drawn: establishing the Church's worship and pastoral care where they do not exist, civilising frontiers, emergency relief, pioneering education, medical care and many other forms of service without 'strings'. Both are essential. Their relationship was clarified at a South African congress on mission and evangelism early in 1973 by a member of the USPG Council, Douglas Webster:

> All evangelism is mission. Not all mission is evangelism. . . .
> Healing, teaching, baptizing, liberating, protesting, working for peace and justice, feeding the hungry, reconciling those at variance, are all essential parts of mission. . . . Evangelism is the proclaiming of the Gospel, particularly to those who have not heard it, or who have not understood it, or who have not responded to it, or who have forgotten it.[5]

That Gospel proclaims what *God* does through the life, death, resurrection, ascension and second coming of Christ and the sending of his Holy Spirit, and calls for the human response of repentance and faith. Evangelists are God's witnesses, not his agents.

New kinds of mission have always been suspect: women missionaries, medical work, ecumenical co-operation in South India had for many years to be supported by SPG in devious ways. The changes taking place in the Society's work today are mostly the realisation of forgotten aspects of our own inheritance. Some, for example, think USPG's involvement in home mission a questionable innovation, but as Morgan points out, the past shows SPG as performing a vital service to the Church *in this country* and even its greatest achievements overseas do not eclipse this fact. . . . I believe the Society has the same function today. SPG has proved not only a goad pricking the home Church into a missionary awareness but also, through its work, has been able to show the home Church a little more of the lineaments of its own true countenance.[6]

The debate about the role of voluntary societies within the Church has also been around at least since the 1820s.

SPG's growth was as *ad hoc* as that of the British Empire. It ought not to disturb us that the propagation of the Gospel in modern times has gone hand in hand with trade and empire. St Paul took the Gospel along trade routes and Roman military roads to the great cosmopolitan commercial cities of the world he knew: proud of his citizenship, he did not hesitate to invoke the protection of an empire many thought cruelly oppressive. It was probably Christian traders who first brought the Gospel to Britain; the first English martyr was a Roman soldier; Pope Gregory got the idea for his English mission in a Roman slave-market. We have no cause to be ashamed that, in the providence of God, the British Empire—in spite of all, the most benevolent the world has ever known—made possible the spread of the Gospel through a wider world than St Paul dreamt of.

Today we hear the Great Commission with different ears. Anthropological and psychological insights open to us dimensions of the Biblical message unperceived by earlier messengers. Those two great modern Hebrew prophets, Marx and Freud, have made us uneasily aware of motives for mission less respectable than those we like to declare. Two world wars have shattered Western complacency and any illusions the Third World ever had about European superiority in anything but the technology of power. All human efforts are ambivalent (including revolutions for 'liberation'): by all means let us humbly confess our failures, but let us also thankfully affirm what God can accomplish through his earthen vessels.

I am particularly grateful to the Society for Promoting Christian Knowledge (SPCK), SPG's elder sister, for permission to quote from a number of books published by them; and to USPG itself for a vast amount of published and unpublished material, including (in addition to quotations indicated in the text) certain passages adapted from my *Starting From Here*, the USPG 1972 Report, from an essay written for the College of the Ascension *Jubilee News-letter* in 1973, and from my *Thinking Mission*, a quarterly commentary experimentally launched in 1974. Within USPG (of whose Association of Missionary Candidates I was privileged for six years to be Warden) I owe much to colleagues too numerous to mention, but my special thanks go to Home Secretary John Dixon for much information and careful comment, and to Isobel Pridmore and Brenda Hough, successive Archivists, whose ability to ferret out *exactly* what one wants from ten tons of Society archives borders on the psychic.

The straitjacket of allotted space compels ruthless, sometimes arbitrary, selectivity. Those wishing a more definitive history should consult (for SPG down to 1951) H.P. Thompson's *Into All Lands* and (for UMCA down to 1957) the official *History of the Universities' Mission to Central Africa* by Anderson-Morshead (Vol. I) and Blood (Vols. II and III), to both of which my debt is very great. I can only bring out of the treasury a very personal selection of things new and old.

One can perhaps apply to USPG some words from an auto-biographical typescript by Herbert Kelly of Kelham, founder of the Society of the Sacred Mission—itself born of an SPG-supported mission to Korea:

> No worker stands wholly apart from his work . . . nor does God's messenger stand apart from his message. . . . The work and the message are part of the man himself. Both have to be learnt, and are never learnt completely.

July 1974

Margaret Dewey

THE EIGHTEENTH CENTURY:

'Come over and help us' (Acts 16.9)

A ship under sail, making towards a point of land, upon the Prow standing a Minister with an open Bible in his hand. People standing on the shore in a Posture of Expectation, and using these words, *Transiens Adjuva Nos.*

—description of the Seal of SPG as adopted in 1701

The Mission of the Establishment

*Missionary motives–A country parson
and his friends–Into action at home and overseas
How to be a missionary*

> Our Lord Jesus Christ, a little before his departure, commissioned his apostles to *Go* and *teach all nations*; or, as another evangelist expresses it, *Go into all the world, and preach the Gospel to every creature.* This commission was as extensive as possible, and laid them under obligation to disperse themselves into every country of the habitable globe, and preach to all the inhabitants without exception or limitation.

THUS THE GREAT pioneer Baptist missionary William Carey opens his *Enquiry into the Obligations of Christians to use means for the Conversion of the Heathens.* This book, published in 1792, launched the modern missionary movement from Britain [1] which brought forth in quick succession the Baptist Missionary Society (1793), the non-denominational London Missionary Society (LMS, 1795), and USPG's great Evangelical partner, the Church Missionary Society (CMS, 1799). That SPG had been at work for ninety-one years when Carey wrote is a measure of how far ahead of its time the Venerable Society was. It was also of its time: behind Carey's second sentence lie SPG's restriction by its Charter to dominions of the British Crown and its greater apparent concern for British emigrants than for 'the Heathens'.

SPG was called into being to fill a spiritual and cultural vacuum in the American colonies, where the veneer of civilisation was proving dangerously thin. Except in Puritan Massachusetts, children were growing up illiterate and undisciplined. Governor Morris of New Jersey wrote that apart from a few Quakers

> the People are generally of no Religion, the Youth of the whole Province are very debauch'd and very ignorant and the Sabbath day seems there to be set apart for Rioting and drunkenness.[2]

Our own kith and kin were scattered abroad as sheep without a shepherd: overseas mission was an extension of home mission.

It is often said that the first Protestants to proclaim evangelisation the duty of the Church as such (not just a colonial responsibility) were the Moravian Brethren, active overseas missionaries from 1732.[3] (Their missionary zeal merged with Pietist spiritual renewal in the Evangelical movement which inspired Carey.) Yet already in 1704 SPG's first full-scale Annual Report affirms that

> the *Propagation of the Gospel in Foreign Parts*, as it is an affair of the highest importance to Mankind, and therefore first given in Charge to his Apostles by the *Son of God* when He commanded them to *Go, Teach and Baptize all Nations in the Name of the Father, of the Son and of the Holy Ghost*: so hath it been the chief Care of Apostolical Men in all Ages downwards, to execute that Commission for the Good of Souls, and the Honour of their Blessed Redeemer.

As in all human endeavour, motives were mixed, but concern for evangelisation of America's aboriginal Indians and African slaves was fundamental to SPG from the start.

Thomas Bray was born in 1658, the studious only son of a poor Shropshire farmer who managed to send him to Oxford. Ordained in 1681, Bray became a Warwickshire vicar and close friend of the saintly Non-Juror John Kettlewell, whose patrons were the Digby family. In 1690 William, Lord Digby, presented Bray to the living of Sheldon. A strong churchman, Digby was Bray's lifelong friend and in due course a member of SPG. It was he who commissioned the portrait of Bray which now hangs in USPG House.

Born in the year of Oliver Cromwell's death, Bray grew up during the Restoration. In his youth, the moral sense implanted in England by the Puritans was reacting sharply to Charles II's loose-living court. Keen young laymen formed societies for cultivating spiritual life under a rule and for reform of manners and morals. Behind the 'permissive society' Bray saw lack of Christian teaching. It was his *Catechetical Lectures*, published in 1696, that brought this young country parson to the notice of the Bishop of London.

Henry Compton, youngest son of the Earl of Northampton and erstwhile tutor to the princesses Mary and Anne, became Bishop of London in 1675. The following year came a *cri de coeur* from John Yeo in Maryland,[4] where there were 'at least 20,000 soules, and but three Protestant ministers of us that are conformable to the doctrine and discipline of the Church of England.' In Maryland the Church had

> many profest enemies, as the Popish Priests and Jesuits are, who are incouraged and provided for. And the Quaker takes care and provides for those that are speakers in their conventicles. But noe care is taken, or provision made, for the building up Christians in the Protestant Religion, by means whereof not only many dayly fall away either to Popery, Quakerism, or Phanaticisme, but also the Lord's Daye is prophaned, religion despised, and all notorious vices committed; so that it is become a Sodom of uncleannesse, and a pest-house of iniquity.

Religious pluralism was then unthinkable: the only question was what should be established. SPG's Royal Charter would launch the mission of the Church of England; in Massachusetts the Establishment was Puritan; anathema to both were the egalitarian Quakers, the 'communists' of the day; behind 'Popery' always loomed England's colonial rival, France. Established Churches represent the ideal of Christendom, with religious conformity as the cultural cement of society. Nonconformity was illegal in England until 1689; when Yeo wrote, Dissent meant sedition.

11

Reports like Yeo's stirred Compton to investigate. Finding his overseas jurisdiction vague, he obtained from Charles II fresh authority over English colonies and 'factories' (trading posts) and £20 passage money for any priest or schoolmaster. This news stirred the colonists to begin building churches, and in 1696 Maryland asked for a commissary.

Offered the appointment, Bray accepted and began at once to seek priests for the colonies. One, sent to Philadelphia, in two years increased his flock from fifty to 700, then died of an illness caught while visiting the sick. Another, similarly successful in South Carolina, died within three years. The harvest truly was plenteous, but the field was perilous and the labourers, understandably, few. Bray could only recruit poor clergy, who could not afford to buy books. So he set about providing libraries, the indispensable foundation of intellectual life on the frontier.[5]

In 1698 he drafted a very broad scheme for Propagating Christian Knowledge at home and overseas. This proved too ambitious, but it led Bray and four keen young lay friends to launch the Society for Promoting Christian Knowledge (SPCK) as a voluntary society. The four were Lord Guilford, 26-year-old son of the Lord Chancellor and himself future President of the Board of Trade; Sir Humphrey Mackworth, barrister and future MP for Cardiganshire; John Hooke, barrister and future Chief Justice; and Colonel Maynard Colchester, future MP for Gloucestershire. They were joined by 33-year-old John Chamberlayne, a brilliant scholar and linguist who became a Fellow of the Royal Society and gentleman-in-waiting to Prince George of Denmark, Queen Anne's consort. Chamberlayne was Secretary of SPCK.

This little 'cell', noting that 'the growth of vice and immorality is greatly owing to gross ignorance of the Christian religion', undertook 'to meet together, as often as we can conveniently, to consult . . . how we may be able by due and lawfull methods to promote Christian Knowledge.'[6] Meet they did, sixty times the first year, expanding their aims and electing new members, among them a young Oxford don named White Kennett. They planned 'charity schools' (the first attempt at mass education for the poor), libraries, printing and distributing literature, support for Bray's overseas efforts, moral improvement of public life, prison reform, and co-operation with Protestants on the Continent, where their correspondents included the Pietists Philip Spener and Augustus Francke. Mission at home and abroad was seen as one.

Bray sailed for Maryland in December 1699. Six months later he was back, convinced that the colonial task called for a larger and more official society. He discussed his new project with Compton, with Archbishop Tenison (who shared Bray's concern for schools and libraries), and at SPCK meetings. On 13 March 1701 it was presented to Convocation, which appointed a committee 'to inquire into Ways and Means for promoting Christian Religion in our Foreign Plantations.' Two days later the committee met and recommended that Bray petition King William III. The petition favourably acknowledged, Bray drafted a Charter which was read and amended at three successive SPCK meetings:

> Wee are credibly informed that in many of our Plantacons Colonies, and Factories beyond the Seas . . . the Provision for Ministers is very mean. And many others . . . are wholy destitute.

Eleven years after the Battle of the Boyne, His Majesty's motives are predictably mixed:

> Many of our Loveing Subjects doe want the Administration of God's Word and Sacraments, and seem to be abandoned to Atheism and Infidelity and alsoe for Want of Learned and Orthodox Ministers to instruct Our said Loveing Subjects in the Principles of true religion, divers Romish Preists and Jesuits are the more incouraged to pervert and draw over Our said Loving Subjects to Popish Superstition and Idolatry.

The Society's twin purposes are

> that a sufficient Mainteynance be provided for an Orthodox Clergy to live amongst them, and that such other Provision be made, as may be necessary for the Propagation of the Gospell in those Parts.

On 16 June the Great Seal of England was affixed to the Charter, and the Society for the Propagation of the Gospel in Foreign Parts was born.[7]

SPG's ninety-six original 'Incorporated Members' included most of the members of SPCK, an assortment of senior clergy (who were no mere figureheads), and sundry peers, gentry and other leading laymen. Archbishop Tenison, as President, nearly always chaired the monthly meetings which determined Society policy and conducted its business. Between meetings, an unofficial group of London members, ancestor of the Standing Committee, was asked to look up details and draft recommendations.

The first meeting, attended by fifteen clergy and fifteen laymen, elected a layman, John Chamberlayne, as the Society's Secretary. The second approved the Society's seal and adopted by-laws and standing orders, providing among other things for an Annual Sermon before the Annual Meeting. According to the first such, preached at St Mary-le-Bow (at 8 a.m.!), SPG missionaries were

> to settle the State of Religion as well as may be among our *own People* there, which by all accounts we have, very much wants their Pious care: and then to proceed in the best Methods they can towards the *Conversion* of the *Natives*.

Copies of the Charter were sent to the dioceses with a letter inviting subscriptions. The response that first year totalled £1,537 —equivalent to perhaps twenty times that amount today. Year by year the Annual Sermon was distributed, with a review of the previous year's work, to the parishes and dioceses of England and Wales. Thus began the Annual Reports which to this day inform the home Church and appeal for prayer, money and offers of service.

There were then no regular collections in church. The Society relied for regular income entirely on members' subscriptions, voluntary gifts and legacies. Another source of funds was the 'Royal Letter', an occasional appeal for some charitable cause: addressed by the Crown to the Archbishops, it directed that on the appointed Sunday 'the Ministers in each parish do effectually excite their parishioners to a liberal contribution',[8] taken up in a house-to-house collection the following week. During SPG's eighty years in America, six Royal Letters on its behalf brought in a total of £65,110—over a million pounds in modern terms.

William III died early in 1702. A loyal Address to Queen Anne brought from that dedicated churchwoman the gracious reply: 'I shall be always ready to do my Part towards Promoting and incouraging so Good a Work.' She was as good as her word. Had she lived longer, the history not only of SPG but of the American colonies might have been very different.

SPG's Charter entrusted to its spiritual care the English trading communities in Europe and overseas. In 1702 grants were made to chaplains in Amsterdam and Moscow. Anglican chaplaincies in Europe were to remain a Society responsibility until 1973.

Letters of inquiry to the colonies brought a flood of appeals. In the West Indies a few small grants were made, but the Church was already established there. On the mainland, the Church was established in Virginia; Maryland's immediate needs had been met by Bray; of the rest, little was known except that north of Philadelphia there were Anglican churches only in New York and Boston.[9]

Informants in London included George Keith. This formidable Scot, mighty in the Scriptures, had been a friend of William Penn and for fifteen years a Quaker missionary in America, until distrust of 'inner light' led him into controversy and in 1700, at the age of sixty-two, to ordination in the Church of England. It was clear that a systematic survey was needed, and that Keith was the man for the job. On 24 April 1702 he sailed for Boston in HMS *Centurion*—the Society's first missionary. The *Centurion*'s chaplain, John Talbot, was so impressed with Keith and his mission that he asked to be allowed to join him.

For two years the pair preached their way from Maine to Carolina and back, discovering where there were enough Church members to support a priest. SPG's aim from the start (not always achieved) was to supplement local effort and build up the local Church as quickly as possible to full self-support. Typically, the local congregation would provide church, parsonage and a minimum stipend; the Society would find the priest and give him an outfit allowance, his fare, a chest of books, and a grant to supplement his salary. The diarist John Evelyn recorded 19 June 1702 that being elected a member of the Society lately incorporated for the Propagation of the Gospel in Foreign Parts, I subscribed £10 *per annum* towards the carrying it on. We agreed that every missioner, besides the £20 to set him forth, should have £50 *per annum* . . . till his settlement was worth to him £100 *per annum*.

Among the Southern plantations the Church quickly took root. In 1759 SPG withdrew from South Carolina and transferred its help to new work elsewhere. In the North, Anglicans were a small and often embattled minority, and SPG help for many parishes continued right up to the War of Independence.

The search for missionaries began. Bishops were asked to commend overseas service to their clergy. Asked what sort of men America needed, Keith said they should be

men of Solidity and good Experience as well as otherwise qualified with good learning and good natural parts and especially exemplary in Piety, and or a discreet Zeal, humble and meek, able to endure the Toil and Fatigue they must expect to go through both in mind and body, not raw young men, nor yet very old, whose Godly Zeal to propagate true Christianity in life and Practice should be their great Motive, for People generally of those parts are very sharp and observant to notice both what is good and bad in those who converse among them.[10]

Keith's stress on witness by personal example is reflected in the instructions drawn up for Society missionaries.[11]

While waiting for passage, missionaries should live 'not in any Publick House, but at some Bookseller's, or in other private and reputable Families' and should 'employ their Time usefully, in Reading Prayers,[12] and Preaching, as they have Opportunity, in hearing others Read and Preach; or in such Studies as may tend to fit them for their Employment.'

During the voyage they should try to be 'remarkable Examples of Piety and Virtue to the Ship's Company', see that daily Prayers and Sunday 'Preaching and Catechizing' are arranged, and 'Instruct, Exhort, Admonish, and Reprove' (as opportunity offers) 'with such Seriousness and Prudence, as may gain them Reputation and Authority.'

In their parishes they are to be 'circumspect and unblameable, giving no offence either in Word or Deed', and to see 'that their ordinary Discourse be grave and edifying . . . and that in their whole Conversation they be Instances and Patterns of the Christian Life.'

Sermons should be on 'the great Fundamental Principles of Christianity, and the Duties of a sober, righteous and godly life, as resulting from these Principles.' Regular visiting of all parishioners is enjoined,

> those of our own Communion, to keep them steady in the Profession and Practice of Religion as taught in the Church of England; those that oppose us, or dissent from us, to convince and reclaim them with a Spirit of Meekness and Gentleness.

Evangelisation of 'heathens and infidels' should, in the new eighteenth-century manner,

> begin with the Principles of Natural Religion, appealing to their Reason and Conscience; and thence proceed to shew them the Necessity of Revelation, and the Certainty of that contained in the Holy Scriptures, by the plainest and most obvious Arguments.

Twice a year each missionary had to send the Society a detailed report with statistics of baptisms, communicants, population and general information about the colonial situation. The 50,000 pages of SPG missionaries' reports from America, neatly bound in the USPG Archives Room, have been called 'the finest body of exact information on all subjects that exists in the English language for the eighteenth century.'[13]

CHAPTER TWO

Building Christendom in a New World

---

*The people of the land—The black proletariat
'We have great need of a bishop here.'
Ecumenical co-operation in South India
Codrington's dilemma—A change of climate
Yankee missionaries—Of pubs and prisoners and
a 'failed' missionary—Mid-century initiatives*

KEITH'S SURVEY began in Boston, where a sermon of his started a pamphlet war. Many New Englanders were welcoming, but the Massachusetts Puritans would again and again exert political pressure in London to block every SPG attempt to found an American bishopric. In New York, then a town of 16,000, Keith and Talbot were welcomed by William Vesey, energetic young rector of Trinity Church and commissary for the Bishop of London. Vesey, wholly supported locally, was never an SPG missionary, but was its trusted adviser until his death in 1746. He was greatly concerned about the Indians and Negro slaves, and SPG's most fruitful work among both was done in his area.

At Albany, 150 miles north of New York, conferences were being held with the Mohawks, one of the Five (later Six) Nations of the Iroquois Confederacy which stood between the English and the 'Papist' French to the north. The New York-to-Canada water route, hostile control of which would split the colonies, ran through Mohawk lands. The Mohawks, suspicious of the French and their Jesuit missionaries, asked the English for 'some to teach them religion'. In 1704 SPG sent them Thorogood Moor.

The Albany whites were a mixed lot: Dutch burghers, an English garrison, fur traders who gave the Indians 'fire water' in order to swindle them more easily. Lord Cornbury, the Governor, said Moor's fortnightly celebration of Holy Communion was 'too frequent' and imprisoned Moor when he persevered! The Mohawks Moor found friendly but noncommittal:

> 'Tis from the behaviour of the Christians here that they have had and still have their notions of Christianity, which God knows has been and is generally such that I can't but think has made the Indians even hate Christianity.[1]

Massachusetts was then paying a bounty for every Indian scalp, and its population explosion was causing younger sons to cast envious eyes at the red man's land further west. Mission to the whites was clearly urgent, and in 1708 SPG started work among them in Albany.

In 1710 four Mohawks came to London, were presented to Queen Anne, who gave a silver Communion service for 'her Indian Chappel of the Mohawks'. To SPG they repeated in person their request for Christian teaching. Jolted out of preoccupation with colonists, the Society promised two missionaries and resolved

> that the design of propagating the Gospel in foreign Parts does chiefly and principally relate to the conversion of heathens and infidels; and therefore that branch of it ought to be prosecuted preferably to all others.

Four years later our man among the Mohawks, forty-four miles northwest of Albany by forest track, complained that in winter

> we can scarce stir abroad by reason of the Extreme Cold-ness of the Weather and deep Snows, and in Summer tormented by fflyes and Muschetoes, and can't stir abroad without being in danger of being stung with the Snakes, here are so many of them, Especially the Rattlesnake.[2]

He improved his time by translating the Prayer Book into Mohawk. A generation later most Mohawks in the area were Christians.

In its mid-century Mohawk work, SPG relied greatly on Sir William Johnson. This Irish-born country gentleman and adopted Mohawk found ordinands, got churches and parsonages built, even offered 20,000 acres to endow an Albany bishopric. One of his ordinands was John Stuart, six-foot-four son of a Scottish Covenanter, who, duly ordained in London, took up the Mohawk work in 1770. Much of the War of Independence was fought over that strategic Mohawk waterway. Stuart, imprisoned as a Loyalist, wrote that

> all the Mohawks, being loyal, were obliged to desert their habitations and fly back to the Wilderness to avoid the fury of the Rebels . . . My House has been frequently broken open by Mobs, my Property plundered, and indeed every kind of indignity offered to my Person by the lowest of the Populace . . . My Church was plundered by the Rebels (and) afterward imployed as a Tavern.[3]

Released in 1781, Stuart made his way to Tyenderoga in Upper Canada (modern Ontario), where his faithful Mohawks welcomed him. Another group had settled on the Grand River; SPG built churches for both. Queen Anne's Communion plate, buried when they fled, was recovered, divided between the two, and is still in use.

SPG's work among Africans began in 1703 with a letter from Elias Neau, a French trader in New York. Now one of Vesey's parishioners, Neau had for his Huguenot faith once spent seven years as a French galley-slave. It did not then occur even to an ex-slave to question the institution of slavery, but New York's Negroes, Neau insisted, were entitled to education and baptism. He asked SPG to send a catechist.

Who better, replied the Society, than Neau himself? He started a night-school. Vesey urged his parishioners to send their slaves. At first few did so: educated blacks might get awkward ideas, and might not baptism free them from slavery as well as from sin? Vesey and Neau got the Assembly to pass an Act expressly denying this, and the school grew. A slave riot in 1712 was wrongly attributed to Neau's pupils; when the trial revealed the true culprits, Governor Hunter, himself a member of SPG, sent his own slaves to be taught and publicly proclaimed the duty of educating Negroes.

After Neau's death in 1722 SPG sent a succession of priests to carry on. Most SPG missionaries had to combine Negro work with care of colonies. From 1725, all were specifically charged with instructing and baptizing Negroes in their parishes.

In 1703 Talbot wrote exuberantly that 'we have gathered several hundreds together for the Church of England' and that 'churches are going up amain, where there never were any before.' But one plea runs through his reports like a refrain:

> We have great need of a Bishop here, to visit all the churches, to ordain some, to confirm others, and bless all. . . . The poor Church has nobody on the spot to comfort or confirm her children; nobody to ordain several that are willing to serve, were they authorised, for the work of the ministry. Therefore they fall back again into the herd of dissenters, rather than they will be at hazard and charge to go as far as England for orders.[4]

The charge was £100 return; the hazard, that one in five perished in the attempt. It took Hebron, Connecticut, twenty years to get a priest: their first candidate drowned; the next died of smallpox; the third was taken prisoner by the French; the fourth also caught smallpox, but lived to become their rector.

The colonial Church was theoretically under the Bishop of London, but he never visited it, and his commissaries were few and far between. SPG exercised such supervision as there was, through correspondence and through key men on the spot, ordained and lay, like Vesey and Johnson. Some colonial Governors were keen Churchmen and of great assistance. Thus in the providence of God an episcopal Church with neither bishops nor unifying structures was planted from Newfoundland to Georgia and held together for eighty years.

SPG's 1704 Report was widely distributed. Surveying each field of work, the help already given and the many unfulfilled requests, it ended with an urgent appeal for men and money. News of the Society's founding had already stimulated Continental missionary activity. The Danish king sought missionaries for his South Indian colony of Tranquebar. No Danes would volunteer, so in 1706 he sent two Germans from the Pietist university at Halle. Their first report, translated into English, was dedicated to SPG and circulated by it in England.

SPG could not support work outside British dominions nor by other than 'an orthodox clergy', but Bray and his friends put on their SPCK hats and sent a printing-press, on which the first Tamil New Testament was printed. When the mission spread and the Danish Crown refused support outside its territory, SPCK took over. No English clergy would go, so SPCK, too, turned to Halle. It was with German Lutherans that for more than a century SPCK staffed the 'Danish' mission as it spread northward through Madras and Tinnevelly.

What does a committed Christian do, given vision beyond his time and vested interests beyond his power to dislodge? In 1698 Christopher Codrington, gentleman scholar and Fellow of All Souls, inherited the family estates in Barbados and became Governor of the Leeward Isles. On the 'sugar islands'—chief source of England's growing wealth—life for planters was affluent and easy-going; the Established Church was the plantocracy at prayer. Unlike most planters, the Codringtons had always treated their Negroes well. Now Governor Codrington weighed his wider responsibilities for 'our poor slaves':

> I shall certainly be opposed by all the Planters in generall if I should go about to secure their limbs and lives by a law (though I shall certainly recommend something of that kind), but much more if I should promote the baptising of all our slaves: 'tis certain the christening of our Negroes without the instructing of them would be useless . . . and 'tis evident the few and very ill-qualified clergymen who goe to the Islands are not only insufficient for such work, but can doe noe service to the whole Heathens they find there.[5]

But he had seen dedicated Jesuits at work in the French parts of St Kitts.

> A work of this nature is only fit for regular clergy who are under vows of poverty and obedience. If the Archbishops and Bishop of London can find such a number of apostolical men, who are able to take much pains for little reward, my protection and countenance shall not be wanting.[5]

22

Francis Le Jau, a former Huguenot placed by Codrington in charge of three parishes on St Kitts, found the slaves

> generally sensible and well disposed to learn, but it is the Barbarity of their masters which makes 'em stubborn, not only in not allowing them victuals or Cloaths, but cruelly beating 'em . . . If a Minister proposed the Negroes should be instructed in the Christian Faith, have Necessarys, etc., the Planters are very angry and answer it would consume their profit.[6]

They gave the usual argument that baptism would set Negroes free. Le Jau perceived the real objection: 'they would be obliged to look upon 'em as Christian brethren, and use 'em with humanity.'

Did Codrington despair of change in his lifetime? He knew the mood of the English upper classes. In 1703 he wrote his will, entrusting his estates and his dilemma to the infant SPG. The following year, only thirty-six years of age, he retired from public life. Six years later he was dead.

Thus in 1710 SPG found itself a slave-owner and charged with mission to the whole man. The plantations were to be

> continued intire, and 300 Negroes at least always kept thereon, and a convenient number of Professors and Scholars maintained there, all of them to be under vows of poverty and chastity and obedience, who shall be obliged to study and practice Phisick and Chirurgy as well as Divinity, that by the apparent usefullness of the former to all mankind they may both endear themselves to the people and have the better opportunities of doing good to men's souls whilst they are taking care of their bodys.[7]

The day of Anglican missionary brotherhoods was not yet, but that very year the Society was pondering how to train missionaries in the Caribbean, where education of any kind was almost non-existent. In 1713 it sent a priest-doctor, Joseph Holt—SPG's first medical missionary—to teach and care for the Codrington Negroes. In 1745—many bad harvests and hurricanes later—it opened Codrington School; in 1760 the first of its scholars was ordained.

Why did the Society not emancipate its slaves? There were the terms of the Trust, not easy to break. No planter would then have followed such an example, whereas humane treatment within the system was at least within their ken. Forced labour (of convicts, children, impressed seamen) was taken for granted. And the tide was running against reform: in 1713 England acquired the monopoly of the slave trade. In such a society, the last state of a freed Negro (with no legal rights whatever) could well be worse than the first.

The solution to Codrington's dilemma would involve political action at the seat of power to overturn the institution of slavery itself. 'It is fair to claim that the pastoral care of the Church at last created the conscience which saw the wrong in slavery',[8] but in the early eighteenth century nobody but a few Quakers was sufficiently detached from the Establishment to think the unthinkable.

SPG's efforts to establish an American bishopric were going well when in August 1714 Queen Anne died, followed in 1715 by Archbishop Tenison, whose personal enthusiasm had meant so much. Tenison hopefully bequeathed £1,000 towards endowing two colonial bishoprics, but the climate had changed.

The Hanoverian Georges cared neither for bishops nor for the propagation of the Gospel. Whig politicians anxious to appease Dissent listened to New England Puritans. Bishops were now 'safe' men of Latitudinarian theology, and in 1717 Convocation was suspended lest the Lower House rock the boat. Politics was corrupt. Memories of religious wars encouraged the new faith in human reason. 'Enthusiasm' became a dirty word. Tolerance, now a virtue, was barely distinguishable from indifference. Individual bishops continued to back the missionary efforts of a few keen clergy and laity, but SPG's link with the Establishment began to prove a mixed blessing.

In 1710 some Anglicans in Stratford, Connecticut, petitioned the Crown for their rights, the Bishop of London for a priest, and SPG with a long tale of woe. For years these Connecticut Yankees had been persecuted by the Congregational authorities for nonconformity. The last straw was being forced (by the imprisonment of their churchwarden) to support a Congregational minister and the building of his house.

It was twelve years before the Society could send them a priest. His surprising report was that 'our cause flourishes mightily in this country; indeed, so much so, that our neighbours look on with astonishment.' Well they might: in 1722 Connecticut Congregationalism was shaken to its foundations by the secession to the Church of England of seven of its brightest lights, including the entire staff of Yale College!

One of the strengths of the American Church to this day is the very high proportion of its members whose Anglicanism is a matter of adult conviction and choice. Timothy Cutler, a brilliant young Harvard graduate, had left Stratford in 1719 to become President of Yale. It was he whose house the Churchfolk had been forced to help build. Was it their perseverance which led him to study their Church's doctrine and to resign from high office and ask for Anglican orders? Cutler was to be rector of Christ Church, Boston, for forty-two years.

Samuel Johnson, another of the Yale Seven, was a giant in the colonial Church. SPG sent him to Stratford, where his scholarly reputation drew many a young Harvard and Yale graduate seeking ordination to sit at his feet. Fourteen of Johnson's students, ordained in England, returned as SPG missionaries. Henry Caner became rector of King's Chapel, Boston; Thomas Chandler, a missionary to New Jersey and eloquent advocate of bishops. Samuel Seabury served at New London and then on Long Island; his son (the younger Samuel Seabury, also an SPG missionary) was to be America's first bishop.

In 1712 Chamberlayne resigned as SPG Secretary. His successor was a City type who received letters at St Paul's Coffee House near Chancery Lane. It was in his time that White Kennett, now Dean (later Bishop) of Peterborough, gave the Society his notable collection of books and other material on mission in America.

The third SPG Secretary, a Hertfordshire vicar named Humphreys, operated out of pubs in the Strand ('The Golden Periwig') and Paternoster Row ('The Sun and Bible') until in

1727 the Society hired its first office, in Warwick Court. A poor correspondent, Humphreys did, however, publish in 1730 the first book about SPG, whereupon its income nearly doubled.

1730 also saw the death of its founder, but not before Bray had started yet another society, 'Dr Bray's Associates for Instructing the Negroes in the Christian Religion and Establishing a charitable Colony for the better Maintenance of the Poor of this Kingdom, and for other good Purposes'. Deeply troubled about prison conditions, Bray had arranged in 1727 for SPG missionaries awaiting passage to do prison visiting in Whitechapel and other gaols. It was he who suggested to Oglethorpe the new colony of Georgia as a refuge for the debtors and unemployed who formed so large a proportion of 'convicts'.

The first SPG chaplain in Georgia soon resigned. His successor, a very zealous young priest, arrived in Savannah early in 1736 and promptly 'put his foot in it'. He came home prematurely, a sadder and wiser man who on the long voyage home realised that what he had learnt in the New World was that he was not yet himself converted. His name was John Wesley.

God alone knows what the world he took for his parish owes both to the Methodist movement which ecclesiastical hostility finally drove out of the Established Church and to the Evangelical revival within it. During the corresponding 'Great Awakening' in America, the Church of England's distrust of 'enthusiasm' actually helped its growth: its dignified worship and reasonable doctrine attracted large numbers of thoughtful converts repelled by the emotionalism of revivalist preaching.

Bishop Thomas Secker of Oxford summarised the Society's first forty years:

> Near a hundred Churches have been built: above ten thousand Bibles and Common-Prayers, above a hundred thousand other pious Tracts distributed: great Multitudes . . . of Negroes and *Indians* brought over to the Christian Faith: many numerous Congregations have been set up, which now support the Worship of God at their own Expence, where it was not known before: and seventy Persons are constantly employed, at the Expence of the Society, in the farther service of the Gospel.[9]

In 1749 the Board of Trade and Plantations asked SPG to find priests and schoolmasters for six new towns in Nova Scotia. The Rev. William Tutty and a schoolmaster sailed with the first party to Halifax. Building a community with uprooted people is never easy: some settlers were decent folk, but Tutty found the majority 'a sett of most abandoned wretches . . . deeply sunk into almost all kinds of immorality', with 'scarce a shadow of religion'. Immigrants from strait-laced New England, 'justly scandalised at the barefaced immorality of the others', were not noticeably godly in their own business dealings.

But Tutty got on with the job. St Paul's, Halifax—the first Anglican church in Canada—was built in 1750. The following year Tutty wrote that 'the Colony in general is much amended, and the behaviour of the worst among them is less profligate and abandoned'; best of all, Churchfolk and Dissenters were living 'in perfect harmony'.[10] So soundly were the Nova Scotian communities built that a generation later, when rebellion broke out to the south, they could absorb five times their own number of Loyalist refugees.

Meanwhile Thomas Thompson, a Yorkshireman and Cambridge don who had exchanged scholarly ease for mission in New Jersey, became so concerned for the slaves there that he asked SPG to send him to their West African homeland in 'the coast of Guiney'. In 1752 he arrived at Cape Coast Castle, a slave-trading fort in what is now Ghana. For four years he struggled with the language and with malaria. Seeing the need for indigenous missionaries, he sent three promising African lads to England for SPG to educate. Only one survived, and was ordained in 1765 the first non-European Anglican priest: Philip Quaque.[11]

Quaque was SPG missionary at Cape Coast for fifty years. It was a lonely task. His English wife died in childbirth. His English education alienated him from his own people, and European slave-traders were not the most promising of parishioners. To make matters worse, the SPG Secretaries of those years were very bad at answering letters. ('For these four or five years last,' wrote Quaque in 1771, 'I have waited with Impatiency for a line or two from the Venerable Society.') But this faithful priest persevered, with financial but very little moral support from the

Society, until his death in 1816. His English successor died almost immediately in that 'white man's grave', and the mission was not resumed until the twentieth century.

Concern for higher education led SPG in 1754 to help found King's College (now Columbia University) in New York. Its first Principal was an SPG missionary, Samuel Johnson of Stratford; the Society also gave a 1500-volume library, £500 from its own funds and £6,000 from a special appeal. In 1760, with the help of Bray's Associates, it founded a second Negro school in New York, which, with the original one, flourished until in 1776 both perished, with Trinity Church and rectory, in the flames of revolution.

CHAPTER THREE

Mission and Politics

---

*The gathering storm—The shot heard
'round the world—Mission accomplished
New frontiers to civilise*

WHEN GEORGE III ascended the throne in 1760, England was at her zenith, her colonial supremacy assured by victories over France in India and Canada. Pope's vision of English power and glory, written in 1712, seemed fulfilled:

> Rise, crowned with light, imperial Salem, rise!
> Exalt thy towering head and lift thine eyes!
> See heav'n its sparkling portals wide display,
> And break upon thee in a flood of day.
>
> See barbarous nations at thy gates attend,
> Walk in thy light, and in thy temple bend:
> See thy bright altars thronged with prostrate kings,
> While every land its joyous tribute brings.

New England's founding fathers had seen themselves as Chosen People in their Promised Land; Old England found its model in Solomon, building Jerusalem with the riches of a far-flung commercial empire. It was easy for the comfortable to forget Solomon's worship of other gods, and the forced labour and murderous taxation behind his glory.

The view was different from America, where prosperous merchants and landed gentry were outnumbered by hard-working yeoman farmers, villagers displaced by enclosure, Quaker radicals, transported convicts, and turbulent Ulster Scots who planted the 'Bible belt' and hatred of England right down the Appalachian frontier. Such was the tinder in which sparks from the minds of John Locke and Tom Paine struck fire. SPG missionaries warned of the gathering storm. Many asserted that the steadying influence of American bishops would have prevented rebellion. Who can say? There were hot heads on one side of the Atlantic and block heads on the other.

In 1759 SPG helped the Churchfolk of Cambridge, Massachusetts build Christ Church for the communities across the river from Boston,

> besides providing for the young Gentlemen who are students at the College here, many of whom as they have been brought up in the Church of England, are desirous of attending the worship of it.[1]

Harvard College, founded in 1636, was the intellectual power-house of American Puritanism. Under East Apthorp (scholarly son of a Boston merchant, educated at the other Cambridge) Christ Church began the student work on Harvard's doorstep which still goes on. But, as a recent rector points out,

> the founding of the mission in Cambridge in the immediate neighbourhood of Harvard College and the appointment of so able a man as East Apthorp simply added fuel to the already strong suspicion that the SPG was not only dangerous as the advance agency of the Church of England, but was composed of Tories committed to uphold the increasingly hated Crown.[2]

In 1763 a pamphlet war broke out, involving even the Archbishop of Canterbury. Apthorp braved the mounting hostility as long as he could, then returned to England.

SPG took great care in selecting missionaries: of 353 sent to America, only thirteen had to be dismissed. Apthorp's successor was one who slipped through the net. Henry Caner of Boston soon brought the Society up to date on 'this very bad man':

> I am sorry to acquaint you that Mr Griffith [as he called himself] has turned out the most impudent imposter that I have ever known. His name, he now says and possibly with truth, is Mieux, son of Richard Mieux, a clergyman now

deceased. He is not in orders, but being possessed of Richard Mieux' letters of Orders, had erased the name and altered the date . . .

What occasioned his destruction was his lying and stealing, for both of which he is infamous to a proverb. He has stolen from every house in the Parish where he was intimate . . . When he found himself discovered, he endeavoured to make off, but was taken, and is now in prison, and to have his trial at the session in October.

The Society took no chances with Christ Church's third rector. Winwood Serjeant, a native of Bristol, had been an SPG missionary since 1756 in South Carolina and in Dorchester, Massachusetts. His eight years in Cambridge were among the parish's happiest.

By now, however, missionary political comment was outspoken and urgent. From New Jersey, Chandler warned that, although 'probably the Parliament are able to enforce the Stamp Act, yet should they resolve to do it, a Disaffection of the Colonies . . . will undoubtedly be established.' On 12 March 1774 Serjeant wrote a missionary's-eye-view of Massachusetts politics, referring to the 'Boston Tea Party':

Political commotions run extremely high in Boston, & if not suppressed soon, the whole Province is in danger of being thrown into anarchy and confusion. The populace are almost daily engaged in riots & tumults: on the 7th instant they made a second destruction of 30 chests of Tea, the property of three or four merchants. The House of Representatives have deported the Chief Justice . . . for accepting a salary from home, lately granted by his Majesty. This act of favour is most indecently treated as a direct infraction of the Constitution of the Province, & violation of the peoples right in appointing and supporting their own officers: Such is the language & violence of republican principles! The grand object is an entire freedom from all taxes, duties & restraints from the British Parliament, respecting both their commerce & civil government. What may be the consequences of these growing disturbances is uncertain.

Which must be the understatement of the eighteenth century.

On 19 April 1775 there was fired in Lexington, Massachusetts, the 'shot heard 'round the world'. Six weeks later, with Boston under siege, Caner wrote to SPG that

> Mr Serjeant of Cambridge has been obliged with his family to fly for the safety of their lives, nor can I learn where he is concealed. His fine church is turned into a barracks by the rebels and a beautiful organ that was in it broke to pieces.

The organ-pipes, melted into bullets, were shot at the British in the Battle of Bunker Hill. Serjeant had gone to earth in Newburyport, whence on 3 August he penned to SPG a hasty message full of 'all the horrors of civil war':

> Was obliged to retreat with my family fifty miles in the country, to Kingston in Newhampshire, where I was in hopes of meeting with a peaceful retirement among rural peasants, but my hopes were soon dissipated; the restless spirit of fanaticism renders unintelligent minds more licentious & ferocious. I found it necessary to remove to Newbury where I hope to be protected from the insults of the common people. Have not lost less than three hundred pounds sterling in household furniture, books, &c. destroyed and pillaged.

Four months later the British evacuated Boston, and Caner fled to Halifax.

Churchfolk everywhere were divided. In the South most were rebels (or 'patriots', according to taste). Most Northern clergy, true to their ordination oath, were Loyalists. Many clergy and layfolk were imprisoned for their loyalty, and a few executed. In New York the ailing rector of Trinity retreated to New Jersey, leaving his young curate, Charles Inglis, in charge. Inglis defied both a message from General Washington (a Churchman) that he 'would be glad if the violent prayers for the King and royal family were omitted' (everywhere the test of political allegiance) and a band of rebels who marched in one Sunday with fife and drum and fixed bayonets, but finally closed the church. Young Seabury, now rector of Westchester, was gaoled, but later escaped to New York—the last Loyalist refuge, recaptured by the British after the rebels had burnt and looted it.

As late as 1782, Inglis reported the Church in Connecticut better attended than the Meeting House, since

> preaching the Gospel unadulterated with Politics raised the Esteem and Respect even of their Enemies; whilst the Pulpits of Dissenters resounded with scarcely any Thing else than the furious Politics of the Times, which occasioned Disgust in the more serious and thinking.

But local support dwindled, and SPG could no longer transmit funds. When Cornwallis surrendered, 35,000 Loyalists fled to Canada and many missionaries with them. Others came to England. When the war ended, Inglis—banished as a traitor and his property confiscated—salied with the departing British troops. SPG's mission to America was ended.

The Connecticut clergy had already met, chosen Seabury (who opted to stay) as their bishop, and sent him to Britain to seek consecration—if necessary, from the non-established Episcopal Church of Scotland. Now an American citizen, Seabury could no longer take the oath of allegiance required of English bishops. Parliament dithered; Seabury headed north, and on 14 November 1784 was consecrated by three Scottish bishops in an upper room in Aberdeen.[3]

American hostility to bishops soon subsided. Two more Americans were consecrated at Lambeth in 1787: William White for Pennsylvania and Samuel Provoost for New York. Whom war had divided, Christian commitment now united: White had been chaplain to the Continental Army; Seabury, to a British regiment.

SPG's Charter forbade work in an independent nation. But already in the 1790s a Society for the Propagation of the Gospel in the State of New York was carrying on where the Venerable Society had left off: the Protestant Episcopal Church in the United States of America had begun its own mission. In 1883 its General Convention sent a message to SPG:

> At the close of the first century of our existence as a national Church, we acknowledge with deep and unfeigned gratitude that whatever this Church has been in the past, is now, or will be in the future, is largely due, under God, to the long-continued nursing care and protection of the Venerable Society.

A recent American historian also acknowledges the Society's secular mission:

> The genius of Thomas Bray and his successors lies in their complete understanding of the frontier problem of intellectual poverty in all its ramifications. With superb intelligence, they took steps to remedy this colonial poverty of the mind and soul. No body of men has ever more thoroughly analyzed the spiritual and intellectual needs of a new society. . . . The SPG was the greatest single influence in promoting a humanitarian culture in the English-American colonies. As the organisation specifically charged with the task of building a civilized society, it was as creative in this field as was the East India Company, for instance, in founding a business empire in India.[4]

A third bishop was consecrated with White and Provoost: Charles Inglis, for 'Nova Scotia' which then included New Brunswick and Upper Canada (both largely settled by American Loyalists), Lower Canada (Quebec), Prince Edward Island and Newfoundland. Following the refugees, SPG went on planting the Church among both settlers and Indians in Canada.

Britain could no longer transport convicts to America. Nobody then had any better idea of what to do with the anti-social and inadequate than to remove them as far as possible from polite society. New South Wales, described in Captain Cook's newly published *Voyages*, sounded promising. In 1787 the first convoy sailed for Australia with 750 convicts, 200 soldiers and a Government chaplain named Johnson. SPG and SPCK supplemented his stipend and supplied him with books. Landing at Botany Bay early in 1788, they settled at what is now Sydney. From such an inauspicious beginning grew another great nation and its Church.

The American rebels could not have won without French help, earnestly solicited by Benjamin Franklin at the court of Louis XVI. Thus that unhappy monarch unwittingly ensured his own downfall: with American success, sparks of revolution jumped the Atlantic to the Paris salons, where the same ferment of ideas had been working. In 1789 the mixture exploded, touching off a chain reaction of revolution throughout Europe and Latin America. The impact of the 'shot heard 'round the world' is not yet spent, and USPG is still involved.

THE NINETEENTH CENTURY:

'Go ye into all the world' (Mark 16.15)

CHAPTER FOUR

'Let My People Go'

*Revolution and complacency—Evangelical
initiatives—Emancipation from ignorance—Action in
the Caribbean—East of Suez
Church/Society relationships—The liberation
of the Church and the disestablishment of mission
A martyr in Melanesia*

IN THE LATE eighteenth century the Church of England was at a low ebb. Prelates took their ease among the aristocracy while impoverished curates read dull sermons in near-empty churches. Learned men argued the reasonableness of belief in God, but few allowed it to interfere with business or pleasure. The natural goodness of man was taken for granted, an easy assumption for enlightened gentlemen and a convenient one for romantics like Rousseau, who extolled the 'noble savage' from afar and (at the very moment when SPG was planting the Church's civilising influence in Halifax) denounced civilisation as the root of evil. The Romantic revolt against rational enlightenment seems new and innocent in every generation, and Rousseau's dreams fire the imagination of revolutionaries to this day. The 'blissful dawn' of revolution in France soon faded into terror and tyranny, but dreams die hard.

Until 1807, slave-ships left London, Liverpool and Bristol with manufactured goods for Africa, returning with West Indian sugar and tobacco. The terrible 'Middle Passage' with its human cargo was invisible to most Englishmen, but that triangular trade financed our industrial revolution. In the 1783 SPG Annual

Sermon, Bishop Beilby Porteous said most West Indian planters considered slaves 'mere machines and instruments to work with, as having neither understandings to be cultivated nor souls to be saved.' Like mechanical plantations, the new factories demanded an abstraction called 'labour', detached from human personality and geared to power-driven machines. In whatever form, the mechanisation of men alienates them from their own humanity.

England emerged from the Napoleonic wars the workshop of the world, but unable to employ or feed her exploding population. The unemployed and dissatisfied streamed overseas to the Promised Lands of Canada and Australia, South Africa and New Zealand. With SPG's help, the Church would go with them.

But not just yet. For forty years the Society drifted under a genial Secretary, Dr William Morice ('a small, square man with a very decided chin but kindly eyes'), whose 'chocolate parties were very agreeable' but who thought colonial bishops 'a troublesome innovation'.[1] In planting the Establishment in Canada, SPG relied increasingly on Government initiative and subsidy: not surprisingly, the idea of self-support proved hard to get across, 'so crippling was the English tradition of a clergy paid by tithes and endowments'.[2]

Bishop Porteous wanted the Codrington estates used to set a new example: to prepare slaves for emancipation through better education, training in responsibility, and allowing 'the most deserving' to work out their freedom, 'all of which could be done without the slightest injury to the rights, the property or the emoluments of the planter.' Though determined 'to end the great evil of slavery', SPG retained as late as 1830 the conviction that *immediate* freedom 'would be followed by more suffering and crime than have ever yet been witnessed under the most galling bondage.'[3] Even Porteous's cautious plan had to wait, for Codrington (plagued by hurricanes) was in a bad way just then.

Through monthly meetings of a few London clergy, the Society disbursed the funds available. In 1793 it began supporting schoolteachers in Australia. But annual income sank, and for thirty-five years no Royal Letter was requested. The 1786 Annual sermon, pleading the needs of India, fell on deaf ears. It was not our finest hour.

But new life was flowing from the mission to Darkest Britain of that 'failed' SPG missionary to Georgia, John Wesley. On the voyage out, Wesley had been much impressed with some Moravian missionaries on the same ship, and on his return placed himself under Moravian spiritual direction. After his conversion, he set out to preach the personal discipleship which is at the heart of all true Christian renewal.

The world Wesley took for his parish was Hogarth's world, and in it Wesley evoked an enthusiasm that frightened the respectable. Christian conversion gave self-respect, and the Methodist 'class meeting' provided group support and moral formation for the neglected lower classes, directing their energies into self-help. The English labour movement had deep Christian roots long before it was politicised by Tom Paine, and before Karl Marx was even born.

Meanwhile the Spirit was working a quiet revival of personal religion among the respectable within the Church. Evangelicals carried the attack on slavery into high places. Granville Sharp instigated the 1772 Mansfield Decision that 'as soon as any slave sets foot on English ground he becomes free'. Thomas Clarkson published his *Essay on the Slavery and Commerce of the Human Species* in 1786, the year of the conversion of the MP for Hull and Yorkshire, William Wilberforce. Clarkson led the agitation around the country (the first successful propaganda effort of the modern sort), Wilberforce in Parliament. In 1807 the slave trade was outlawed. Slavery in the Caribbean did not end till a few days before Wilberforce's death in 1833, but West Africa would no longer be ravaged to supply 'cheap energy' to the plantations.

In 1797 Wilberforce moved to Clapham, joining a group of keen Evangelicals nicknamed 'the Clapham Sect'. By then Carey had published his *Enquiry* and the Baptist and London Missionary Societies were at work. In 1799 sixteen Evangelical clergy and nine laymen (some of them subscribers to SPG and SPCK) resolved that, since

> those respectable societies confine their labours to the British Plantations in America and to the West Indies,[4] there seems to be still wanting in the Established Church a

41

society for sending missionaries to the Continent of Africa, or the other parts of the Heathen world.[5]

They formed themselves into the Church Missionary Society.[6] Space precludes discussion of the principles which differentiate CMS from SPG,[7] but, in addition to being definitely Evangelical, the CMS ethos has always been of the grass roots rather than the Establishment, with a sturdy independence (even from bishops!) in selection and control of its missionaries.

Wilberforce also fought for mission in India. The East India Company maintained chaplains for Europeans, but bitterly opposed attempts at evangelisation, lest Hindu or Muslim hostility upset trade. Charles Simeon, Evangelical vicar of Holy Trinity, Cambridge, inspired a succession of his curates to go out as Company chaplains with the deliberate intention of fostering evangelism. Wilberforce's point of attack was the renewal of the Company Charter every twenty years. In 1793 he tried unsuccessfully to get provision for an Indian bishopric and for missionary work; in 1813, both were achieved.

New life began at last to stir within the Venerable Society, of which Wilberforce became a member in 1800. Much of the stirring was done by Josiah Pratt, energetic Secretary of CMS and an ardent supporter of all mission. Urging SPG to publicise its work more widely, he launched in 1813 an annual *Missionary Register* which included many extracts from SPG Reports. On St Andrew's Day, 1817, Pratt went to Bath for a meeting in aid of CMS. The Archdeacon of Bath angrily protested this intrusion into 'the proper sphere of SPG,' of whose work he painted a glowing if somewhat imaginative picture. *The Times* reported the incident and a pamphlet war followed. This splendid publicity moved SPG to try to justify its new-found reputation.

Renewal came also through a group of dedicated 'High Churchmen' in the tradition which flows through the Caroline Divines, Non-Jurors and Tractarians. This 'Hackney Phalanx' (or 'Clapton Sect') were as keen as the Evangelicals to revive the Church and its mission, but stressed Christ's incarnation rather than his atoning death, and baptism rather than the conversion experience as the foundation of Christian discipleship. Their leader, Joshua Watson, was a layman after Bray's own heart.

Watson's father walked from Cumberland to London at the age of sixteen to escape a farm labourer's life; longing for ordination, he had to settle for working his way from £10-a-year errand boy to wealthy wine merchant. Joshua's elder brother, John, went to Oxford and became Archdeacon of Hackney. Joshua, a cheerful lad destined for the family firm, learnt book-keeping by day, read the classics by night, and left school at fourteen.

Too sensitive not to be troubled by war-time profiteering and inflation, Watson was too conservative to join his friend Cobbett in denouncing the system. He helped destitute workmen to redeem their pawned tools, sought better workhouse conditions for the old, education for the young. In 1814, at forty-three, Watson retired from business to give the whole of his very considerable talents to his Lord in voluntary work. 'More at home on a committee than on a crusade',[8] he immersed himself in the accounts and minute-books of many a voluntary society, several of which he founded. He was to wear more hats than Bray.

Top priority was working-class education. Watson and his friends revitalised SPCK, then in 1811 launched the National Society for Promoting the Education of the Poor in the Principles of the Established Church, with Watson as Treasurer and Andrew Bell as 'Superintendent'. While chaplain at Madras, Bell had developed a system for training the abler pupils to teach the rest,[9] which the National Society adopted. By 1815 its schools were teaching 100,000 children, mostly in industrial areas; twenty years later, nearly a million. The new urban areas being also unchurched, in 1818 Watson helped launch the Incorporated Church Building Society.

On Watson's initiative, SPG inaugurated popular education in Canada. On 21 June 1816 the Society resolved

> that a Committee consisting of the Rev. Dr Wordsworth,[10] Dr Inglis,[11] and Joshua Watson, Esq., be appointed to negotiate with the Committee of the National Society for the purpose of procuring a Schoolmaster, with a view to the introduction of the Madras System of Education into the

North American Colonies, and that they be further authorized to pay the expences of his Voyage to Halifax, and to grant him a competent Salary for three years.

The Rev. James Milne was trained in the new system and sent to Halifax that year, and a Mr West in 1817. By 1820, forty local teachers had been trained, and the system extended to New Brunswick and Quebec.

Moravian, Methodist and Baptist missionaries had long worked among West Indian slaves. Planters bitterly opposed especially 'the dark and dangerous fanaticism of the Methodists'[12] and prevented the Established Church from doing much for Negroes. But in 1818 SPG was at last financially able to implement Porteous's Codrington plan. John Pinder, appointed chaplain to the Negroes, introduced the Madras System into the existing schools and built a new one, together with a hospital (SPG's first), a day nursery, and a chapel.

As the emancipation movement gained momentum in England, SPG again pressed the Government for West Indian bishops, this time successfully. To build up the local ministry, Bishop William Coleridge of Barbados planned with SPG the transformation of Codrington Grammar School into a 'feeder' for Codrington Theological College, opened in 1830 with Pinder as Principal. When illness forced Pinder's return to England in 1835, twenty-seven of his students had been ordained.[13]

In 1830 the Society began emancipating its slaves, allotting them land of their own. Emancipation for all, ready or no, came in 1833. The Government, which paid £20 million compensation to slave-owners, left ex-slaves to fend for themselves. SPG rose to the occasion, launching a Negro Instruction Fund which over the next fifteen years raised and spent £171,777, half of it from the Society's own funds. To stimulate self-help, grants had to be matched locally. £7,000 each went to Mauritius and Bermuda; the rest, to the Caribbean.

Despite the shattered Caribbean economy, the Church's work grew, with SPG help and encouragement toward self-support. By mid-century most West Indians were Christian and a growing proportion literate. But Richard Rawle, then Principal of

Codrington, saw that only through a mission of its own could the lethargic Barbadian Church really be the Church. He longed for a mission to the West African kinsfolk of the ex-slaves. Rousing missionary interest was 'like pulling by the ears a very fat dog, with a strong backward tendency'.[14] But in 1851, on SPG's 150th anniversary, Rawle launched his project as a thank-offering, and the West Indian mission to Gambia and the Rio Pongas was born—the first of SPG's 'grandchildren'.

The rebirth of the Venerable Society coincided with its entry into India. The first diocese east of Suez, styled 'Calcutta', included the entire Indian subcontinent, Ceylon, Penang and (from 1824) Australia. Its first bishop, consecrated in 1814, was Thomas Middleton, one of Watson's friends on the SPCK Committee—a scholarly High Churchman, yet acceptable to Wilberforce. Middleton travelled tirelessly. Impressed with SPCK's work, he urged them to find more missionaries. In Madras, Bombay, Colombo and Penang he founded SPCK branches to supply literature for British troops and seamen and Anglo-Indians, since 'the Gospel has more to fear from the practical atheism of nominal Christians than from the bigotry of ignorant idolaters.'[15]

In 1816 Middleton confided to Watson his doubt

> that the fabric of idolatry in this country will ever be shaken by the preaching of missionaries. My only hope is in the general diffusion of knowledge and the arts as pre-paratory to a feeling of interest about our religion, and then the preaching of missionaries will operate on the minds of the higher classes, without whose concurrence all hope of extensive conversion must be groundless.[16]

The secular education of Hindus and Muslims was thus one aim of the college Middleton founded in Calcutta. Another was training Indian Christians, for 'it is from the labours of ordained converts that we expect the most favourable results.'[17] Other aims were translating Christian literature and orientation of newly arrived missionaries.

This project occasioned Watson's crowning effort to spur SPG into all the world. He quietly set up diocesan SPG Committees, appealed for missionaries, persuaded bishops to attend SPG meetings. Using Middleton's letters, he drafted a memorandum for Archbishop Sutton's use in obtaining a Royal Letter. As SPG's President, Sutton suggested in 1819 'that with the security derived from proper Diocesan control, it now became the Society to step forward with some offer of co-operation with the Lord Bishop of Calcutta.'

At this point dear old Dr Morice was gathered to his fathers and Anthony Hamilton, Morice's assistant for five years, took the helm—a pluralist in the manner of the time,[18] but an effective SPG Secretary nonetheless. Also in 1819 there appeared an anonymous book entitled *Propaganda*: this 'Abstract of the Designs and Proceedings of the SPG, by a member of the Society' (with quotations from SPG Annual Sermons and an eloquent plea for its support) was in fact by the redoubtable Secretary of CMS, Josiah Pratt! The Royal Letter raised £45,747 for Bishop's College; SPG voted £5,000 of its own and CMS, SPCK and the British & Foreign Bible Society similar amounts. The SPG parochial associations set up for this appeal continued to grow and subscriptions to rise, from an annual average of £400 to £51,000 in 1855.

The foundation-stone of Bishop's College was laid in 1820. SPG provided its first Principal and a professor. In its first quarter-century the College laid the foundations of higher education in India, and in 1823 became a centre from which SPG missionaries worked. But fewer than one-third of its students were ordained. In 1880, with SPG help, it was reconstituted as a theological college in more suitable buildings. Its fine tradition of scholarship and spiritual devotion continues to this day to strengthen the Indian Church, and there are still two USPG missionaries on its staff.

Middleton died in 1823, the sheer size of his diocese a death-warrant. His successor, Reginald Heber (the hymn-writer, a Fellow of All Souls, Oxford), was the first to suggest that the missionary societies might unite under official Church patronage. Though nothing came of this, in 1825 Watson engineered the handing over to SPG of SPCK's South India work. The five remaining Lutheran missionaries were maintained, but SPG's 1829 Report notes that

> being a chartered Society, under the presidency of the Primate, its Missionaries are in fact the Missionaries of the Church of England, not of any voluntary association.

Henceforth all new clergy for South India must be in Anglican orders. And at last English clergy began to volunteer.

Heber died in 1826, followed by two more bishops in quick succession, before the Government (prodded officially by SPG and privately by Watson) in 1833 provided bishoprics for Madras and Bombay. Daniel Wilson, an Evangelical with an iron constitution, was consecrated for Calcutta at the age of fifty-three and worked for twenty-five years. Though anti-Tractarian, he agreed with SPG about episcopal authority. This he asserted over both Company chaplains and CMS missionaries—whose control by CMS, pressed by an over-zealous Secretary, elicited from Wilson the comment that 'so far as I understand things at present, the Church Missionary principle, now contended for, extinguishes the Bishop's office.'[19] He battled successfully against caste in the Church and for the legal rights of converts (regarded by Hindus as dead). His church-building campaign culminated in Calcutta Cathedral (1838-46), to which he personally gave £10,000 each for building and chapter endowment; SPG and SPCK each gave £5,000.

So many missionary agencies now appealed to parishes for support that in 1848 Bishop Blomfield of London revived Heber's proposal, but loss of distinctive appeals was rightly feared: 'there were many lukewarm people who would be glad to escape by giving a guinea to one appeal, instead of a guinea each to several!'[20] In the event, CMS at last won the open backing of the archbishops by agreeing to submit future overseas disputes to the home episcopate (in fact there were none), and the principle declared by SPG in 1829 was implemented by the setting up, on SPG initiative, of the Archbishops' Board of Examiners (ABE), appointed by the two English archbishops and the Bishop of London.[21] From 1848, all clergy going overseas through the Society—examined and commended by the ABE—have gone as missionaries of the whole Church of England; in recent years, all USPG-recruited lay missionaries as well.

With the enfranchisement of Dissenters (1828) and Roman Catholics (1829) it could no longer be pretended that Parliament was a lay synod of the Church of England. All Government aid to the Church ceased; disestablishment was in the air. On what could the Church now rely?

In 1833 Watson's friend Hugh James Rose held a conference at Hadleigh rectory in Oxfordshire, John Keble preached his sermon on 'National Apostasy', and Newman's Tracts for the Times began. The High Church movement's centre of gravity shifted to Oxford, but it was Watson who drafted the clergy and lay petitions to the Archbishop of Canterbury, pleading for revival of the ancient disciplines of the Church and the promotion of its purity, efficiency and unity. Bishop Blomfield led the administrative reformation which followed, but Watson made the first draft of the Ecclesiastical Commission of 1836. With two friends he founded the Additional Curates' Society in 1837.

The £12,000 annual Government subsidy for SPG's Canadian work ceased after 1832, and the Society considered withdrawing its missionaries. Watson insisted the Church could raise the money, and himself organised more SPG parochial associations, district committees, and wider circulation of literature. Subscriptions rose steadily and, with a series of Royal Letters[22] and other special appeals, assured the continued expansion of the Society's work.

A new SPG Secretary (1833-43), Archibald Montgomery Campbell,[23] organised deputation tours by six gentlemen (including Watson and Samuel Wilberforce[24]) to solicit subscriptions. A hard-working, methodical man, Campbell established efficient office procedure, began systematic missionary education through literature, appealed to bishops and universities, and himself travelled in the industrial North and in Wales.

In 1829 Watson's friend William Broughton (who had served a City office apprenticeship before a legacy enabled him belatedly to go to Cambridge and seek ordination) was appointed Archdeacon of New South Wales, whose population of 36,500 included

17,000 convicts. With his wife and two daughters he sailed on a convict ship. He found appalling social and moral conditions urgently requiring schools and teachers, churches, parsonages and clergy. In 1834 Broughton came home for help: SPCK gave £3,000; SPG £1,000 and the promise of full support. Consecrated first Bishop of Australia in 1836, Broughton set up local Australian SPG and SPCK committees to collect money, and began building churches. SPG sought volunteers from the universities, offering to add £50 to the £150 Government stipend and to double the £150 passage and outfit allowance; it sent seven men in 1837 and many more thereafter.

The Government would no longer endow overseas dioceses. Broughton's need to divide his (pleaded in London by Watson) led Blomfield to organise in 1841 the Colonial Bishoprics' Fund. His right-hand man and Secretary of the Fund was Ernest Hawkins, former Fellow of Exeter College, Oxford, and now curate of St George's, Bloomsbury, and Assistant Secretary of SPG; the Treasurer was young William Gladstone, a member of SPG's Standing Committee.

First fruit of the Fund was the consecration in 1841 for the new colony of New Zealand of George Augustus Selwyn, a gifted and athletic Etonian who spent the five-month voyage out studying navigation and the Maori tongue, rowed himself ashore at Auckland, and the following Sunday preached in Maori! Of particular significance was the consecration in 1847, at a packed choral Eucharist in Westminster Abbey, of Robert Gray for Cape Town and three others for Australia: previous consecrations of colonial bishops had been hole-in-corner affairs at Lambeth; now the Church was *seen* to send out missionary bishops to plant the Church where it did not yet exist.

On Campbell's resignation in 1843, Hawkins became the first full-time Secretary of SPG, and one of its greatest. Studying the Society archives, he produced new literature, in 1856 launched the monthly *Mission Field* (SPG's chief periodical for eighty-five years) and enlarged the Annual Report. He was the first SPG Secretary to travel overseas (to Canada in 1849). Thirty-nine missionary bishoprics were founded in his time, many of them endowed by SPG special appeals.

Society work expanded rapidly: full-scale help to Ceylon (entered in 1840) in 1845; St Helena in the South Atlantic and Hong Kong, both in 1849; in 1851 the first of a long line of SPG chaplains went to tiny, lonely Tristan da Cunha. In 1853 SPG took over from the Borneo Church Mission (assisted since 1848) full support of the pioneering work of the priest-doctor Francis McDougall and his redoubtable wife, Harriette, among the Dayaks. To Borneo in 1857 SPG sent its first woman missionary (other than wives), Sarah Coomes. In the Indian Ocean it began work in Mauritius in 1855, in Madagascar in 1864; among the Pacific islands, in 1861. Work in Burma began in 1859. In the Crimean war twenty-five SPG chaplains ministered in Florence Nightingale's hospitals and in the field; afterwards the Society helped build Christ Church, Constantinople, for Christian witness in that great Muslim city.

Hawkins retired to a canonry of Westminster in 1864. In his time SPG annual income had risen from £16,557 to £91,203; SPG-linked parishes from 290 to 7,270; missionaries supported from 180 to 493.

Broughton wanted missionary priests trained as such. In 1848, in the ruins of the old missionary monastery at Canterbury, was built St Augustine's college, whence a stream of ordinands of all races was to go forth. Watson helped draft its constitution. He never set foot outside England, but his personal friendship and tireless correspondence with overseas bishops—Middleton of Calcutta, Inglis of Nova Scotia, Hobart of New York, Broughton of Australia, Selwyn of New Zealand—quietly forged links which were forming the Anglican Communion. He found SPG moribund; by his death in 1855, it was indeed going into all the world. If you dig deeply enough into almost any major Society initiative in those years, you find Watson involved, but so self-effacingly that the official historian of SPG's 200th anniversary mentions him but once (in a footnote); the historian of its 250th, not at all.

Broughton wished to assert the spiritual authority of the Church as such. In 1850 he gathered the Australian and New Zealand bishops to discuss a Church constitution. A synod in all but name, this was a landmark in Church decision-making independently of the Crown. The Australian Board of Missions was set up; the following year Sydney and Newcastle dioceses gave Selwyn a schooner for his mission to the Melanesian islands. From its deck Selwyn wrote to SPG that it was its policy in building up colonial Churches which led them to support mission in their turn. In 1854, seeking authority for a constitution for the New Zealand Church, Selwyn visited England: he found, instead, the conviction that the 'consensual compact' of its own members sufficed.

Selwyn soon saw that the Pacific could only be evangelised by islanders. The climate was deadly to Europeans and local suspicion of white men well founded. 'Blackbirding' (kidnapping) of islanders to work on Queensland sugar plantations was understandably seen as a crime to be avenged. Islanders spoke a Babel of languages, and inter-island warfare was chronic. In 1844 Selwyn had (with SPG help) founded St John's College, Auckland, to train white and Maori ordinands together. (As at Codrington, all were to receive simple medical training.) Now he must persuade island boys to train at St John's and return to teach their own people. In view of the usual fate of those lured on to white men's boats, the patience required to win the islanders' confidence can be imagined. But the scheme worked.

In England Selwyn obtained £10,000 endowment for a Melanesian bishopric, an increased SPG annual grant of £300, the ship *Southern Cross* and his fellow-Etonian John Coleridge Patteson. For four years the two cruised together, bringing boys to Auckland for the summer, returning them home in winter (when New Zealand was too cold for them). In 1861 Patteson was consecrated bishop. 'There will never be, perhaps,' wrote Bishop Abraham in the 1867 SPG Report,

> such another man as Bishop Patteson for 300 years to come (it is that time since Xavier) who could learn *ab initio* thirty or forty new languages, and reduce them to writing and grammar and win the hearts of all men of all colours and creeds.

But the 'blackbirding' went on. At the 1871 New Zealand general synod Patteson demanded that this outrage be stopped by law. Later that year he went ashore on Nakapu—and was clubbed to death, in ritual vengeance, by the uncle of five boys recently kidnapped. Patteson's body, pushed off the island in a canoe, bore five symbolic wounds. On his breast was a palm frond tied in five knots: given to SPG and placed in its chapel, this was for a century the Society's most priceless treasure; returned to Melanesia in 1971, it now rests in the new cathedral in Honiara.

The news reached England at St Andrew's-tide. At last the Government stopped the illegal slave trade. SPG, which as early as 1709 had urged an annual day of fasting and prayer for mission, now asked the Archbishop of Canterbury to appoint such a day. The fruits of this observance, first kept 20 December 1872 and subsequently at St Andrew's-tide, have been incalculable.

CHAPTER FIVE

'I Beg to Direct Your Attention to Africa'

Afrikaner Genesis and Exodus—Beginning from
Cape Town—Mackenzie's grave—An island base
From Zanzibar to Lake Nyasa
The Anglican Communion emerges—Up from the south

THE CAPE OF Good Hope was settled in 1652 by the Dutch East India Company. French Huguenots and some Germans followed, but immigration ceased in 1707. In a century of isolation, Afrikaans language and Afrikaner attitudes reached much their present form. Europeans with no taste for hewing their own wood and drawing their own water decided in 1717 to use the slave labour of local Hottentots and imported East Indians. Intermarriage (there being no race prejudice then) produced today's 'Cape Coloured' community.

Moving inland, settlers took their values increasingly from their Church. A narrow, rigidly rational Calvinism, nurtured by divines from the Covenanting Scottish Lowlands, split off and repressed from consciousness the 'pagan' emotional and imaginative side of human nature with its instinctual drives: archetypal 'blackness'. Remote from civilisation, they evolved, like the 'Scotch-Irish' of the American South, a rural white tribalism equally fearful of city sophistication and the disturbing darkness of their new neighbours. For around 1770 Boers seeking wider pastures encountered the Xhosa vanguard of the Bantu, slowly migrating southward from East Africa with *their* cattle. The

53

Tswana stopped in Bechuanaland (modern Botswana); the Barotse, in what is now southwest Zambia. But behind the Xhosa flowed a black tide: Pondo, Griqua, Sotho, Swazi, Zulu. . . . The clash, when it came, was over land.

British settlement of the Cape[1] began in 1820. Next year SPG sent out William Wright and asked the Government 'that permanent means of religious worship and instruction should be at once secured.'[2] Wright founded schools for all races but, opposed for his liberal views, came home in 1829. Anglican work among non-Europeans ceased till 1847. Bishops en route to Calcutta held confirmations and ordinations and deplored the Church's backwardness. Moravians had worked there since 1737; the LMS, since 1799. Methodists and Presbyterians were busy. 'Is it not monstrous', wrote Bishop Turner to Watson in 1829,

> that at the close of 20 years' uninterrupted occupation of
> the Colony . . . we have but one edifice set apart for public
> worship,[3] and that the clergy are only five in number? . . .
> Every denomination of Christians to be found in the
> Colony (and they are pretty numerous) have a place of
> worship in Cape Town, except the Church of England.[4]

The Boers, having missed the European Enlightenment, resented British humanitarian attitudes to 'natives'. In 1835, after British abolition of slavery, the archetypal Exodus of Afrikaner mythology began—the 'Great Trek' into the Promised Land of the interior where, beyond British rule, they would live like Old Testament patriarchs with their flocks and herds. The Matabele, driven out of the Transvaal in 1837, settled in what is now western Rhodesia, dominating the peaceful Shona to the east. A Boer victory over the Zulu at Blood River on 16 December 1838 is still solemnly commemorated as the 'Day of the Covenant'.

Bishop Gray arrived in Cape Town in 1847 with his wife (who fortunately shared his tastes for riding and for disciplined study), two priests, five laymen, three small Government stipends and a £500 SPG annual grant. This former SPG local secretary relied greatly on the Society ('the mainstay of the whole Colonial

Church') as he built the South African Church into an independent province from the Cape to the Zambesi.

In 1848 Gray trekked nearly 3,000 miles, east to Grahamstown, then inland. Next year he sailed to St Helena. In 1850 he went 4,000 miles—north to Bloemfontein, then east across the Drakensberg into Natal, where he pondered Zulu needs. Top priority was a bishop on the spot. Home in 1852, he appealed for bishoprics for Grahamstown and Natal (SPG gave £1,500 for each). Natal's Bishop, John William Colenso, was a brilliant Cambridge mathematician of Cornish Nonconformist upbringing whose missionary greatness was to be clouded by theological controversy. He soon came home to recruit missionaries, returning early in 1855 with forty. Among them (as Archdeacon of Natal) was another Cambridge mathematician, equally gifted but more unassuming, thirty-year-old Charles Frederick Mckenzie.

Home again in 1857, Gray proposed a mission northward from Natal to the Zambesi—to be led, he hoped, by Mackenzie. At this point events were taken out of his hands, for on 4 December, in the Senate House at Cambridge, David Livingstone made his historic appeal to the universities:

> I beg to direct your attention to Africa:—I know that in a few years I shall be cut off in that country, which is now open; do not let it be shut again! I go back to Africa to try to make an open path for commerce and Christianity; do you carry out the work which I have begun. *I leave it with you!*

Livingstone was a self-made rugged individualist. Born into a Blantyre slum, from the age of ten he worked a twelve-and-a-half hour day in a cotton mill. Propping a book on the spinning jenny, he read while working. He attended evening classes, got into medical school, qualified as a doctor. In 1840 he offered himself to the LMS, who sent him to South Africa to join Robert Moffat at Kuruman in Bechuanaland.

As a conventional missionary Livingstone was a failure. Initially shocked that in twenty years Moffat had made but forty converts, in eight years he himself made but one, who soon lapsed. Impatient alike with fellow missionaries and the mission-station system, he found his vocation in opening the interior for others. He married Moffat's daughter, but his family life, too, must be reckoned a failure. His great secular work of exploration and denunciation of the slave trade thus exposed called for a 'loner' of relentless determination, prepared literally to 'leave all' for his Lord's sake. A man of his age in his naïveté about commerce, he was vastly ahead of it in his deep love and respect for Africans as persons and his appreciation of their culture. But unending tribal warfare finally convinced him that for Africa's sake tribalism must be destroyed and Africans civilised.

Livingstone's mission could not be contained by any society or denomination. In 1857 he went home, resigned from the LMS, fired public imagination with his best-selling *Missionary Travels and Researches in South Africa*, and (himself a Scottish Independent) appealed to the ancient universities and Established Church of England to liberate Africa—from slavery, for Christ.

Gray at once backed the new scheme. In 1858 the Oxford and Cambridge Mission to Central Africa was formed[5] to send six or more missionaries, under a bishop—precisely where, was left to Livingstone. On All Saints' Day, 1859, a 'Great Zambesi Meeting' in Cambridge heard Bishop Samuel Wilberforce of Oxford (whose father had led the earlier fight against slavery) affirm that 'England can never be clear from the guilt of her long continued slave trade till Africa is free, civilised, and Christian.'[6]

Mackenzie was offered, and accepted, the headship of the Mission. With him would go his sister Anne, two priests, a carpenter, an agricultural labourer, and a 'lay superintendent'. SPG had worked out from European settlements; UMCA must be self-sufficient in the wilderness. At a great farewell service in Canterbury Cathedral on 2 October 1860, Wilberforce addressed to Mackenzie Moses' parting words to Joshua:

> Be strong and of a good courage, for thou must go with this people into the land which the Lord hath sworn unto their fathers to give them, and thou shalt cause them to inherit it.

Convocation, which Wilberforce was stirring into life, passed a resolution hoping 'that the Bishop of Cape Town and his com-provincials may be able to see fit to admit the head of this Mission into the Episcopal order before he be sent forth to the heathen.' It was thus at the formal request of the Church of England that in Cape Town on 1 January 1861 Mackenzie was consecrated 'Bishop of the Mission to the tribes dwelling in the neighbourhood of the Lake Nyasa and River Shiré.'

Leaving Anne Mackenzie to follow later, the rest sailed on 12 January to join Livingstone at the mouth of the Zambesi. Mackenzie recorded their confidence in a prospect

> which does not depend upon our life or death (nor) upon our successes during our lifetime, but depends entirely upon the grace of God; a prospect which will undoubtedly be realised in God's good time, for we know that 'the knowledge of the Lord shall cover the earth as the waters cover the sea.'[7]

After several weeks of exploring the Ruvuma River (where Mackenzie narrowly escaped being eaten by a crocodile), the two-month voyage up the Zambesi began in May.

> Sometimes the steamer took twenty-four hours to advance twelve miles. It burnt wood, and the wood had to be cut; it stuck on a sandbank, and had to be pushed off. Those who worked it had fever, and so had most of the Mission party; but unfortunately so lightly that it led them to despise the enemy.[8]

Eighty miles inland they turned up the Shiré River. Three missionaries established a base at Chibisa's village; Livingstone and the rest sought a healthier home in the highlands. With Livingstone were some Makololo from Bechuanaland.

> To conquer the land and subdue it for Christ, this little procession set forth, the great Doctor tramping along at the head . . . The Makololo followed, bearing the burdens, including forty days' provisions; lastly came the missionaries, headed by their Bishop

with pastoral staff in one hand and loaded gun in the other, for 'mindful that there was already war in the land, they were all armed.'[9] Eventual UMCA policy was against violence even in self-defence. This pioneering expedition beyond European sovereignty had to act first and think afterwards.

Africans had always enslaved other Africans, and there was a ready market with the Portuguese and the Zanzibar Arabs. Livingstone had been in the area before, but had not grasped the true situation. He had seen Yao prey upon Nyasa, but did not know the Yao were themselves being driven south by the Makua, nor that all lived in fear of the warlike Angoni, a Zulu people pressing northward. Livingstone's chosen mission-field was a no-man's-land, and the missionaries unwittingly took sides in tribal politics.

Eighty-four Nyasa freed by Livingstone from a passing slave caravan became the bishop's first flock. The party settled at the Yao village of Magomero, Livingstone having driven off the Yao.[10] All built themselves thatched huts in the local manner; the Nyasa planted gardens; the missionaries learnt their language. Mackenzie found time to write two learned mathematical papers. In November another priest, Henry Burrup, arrived with a doctor and a shoemaker.

But war brought famine in the land; and with famine, fever. All the missionaries had malaria. On 3 January 1862 Mackenzie started downstream with Burrup and some Makololo boatmen to meet the steamer bringing needed supplies. Ten days later they were travelling by moonlight to escape the mosquitoes on shore when the canoe foundered. Nobody was hurt, but their medicine chest was lost. 'I think I have escaped any ill consequences,' wrote Mackenzie on 13 January. They had stopped in a nearby village.

> I have my hopes that our being here in this way may be intended to prepare the village for being one of the stations to be worked by our Mission steamer (the University boat) for which I hope to write by this mail.
> So matters stand at present. Burrup is very low, and we have no medicine. Quinine, which we ought to be taking every day, there is none. But He who brought us here can take care of us without human means . . . Goodbye for the present.[11]

Mackenzie's last message, about the Mission steamer, was dated 16 January. Of his last fortnight little is known (Burrup was too ill to remember much); malaria claimed him on 31 January.

Burrup buried his bishop and returned to Magomero, where three weeks later he, too, succumbed.

By January 1863 half the Shiré valley had died of starvation. Two more missionaries died; two were invalided home. Magomero was abandoned. Most of the freed Nyasa became villagers of the local Yao chief (who gave, and kept, his promise to protect them); twenty orphans were placed in families in Cape Town. Save for bitter lessons learnt, the Mission seemed a failure. But Mackenzie's grave was the lode-star for future mission into the interior.

Mackenzie's successor (consecrated in Westminster Abbey in February 1863) was William Tozer, the hard-working, bold, bearded vicar of Burgh in Lincolnshire. With him sailed his colleague Edward Steere and another priest-friend, Charles Alington, a deacon, a doctor, a carpenter, a bricklayer, and another artisan. Tozer saw at once the need for a healthier base and, braving all opposition, moved the Mission to Arab-ruled Zanzibar, twenty miles off the coast of Tanganyika. Zanzibar's Swahili tongue is East Africa's *lingua franca*, and the Sultan's sovereignty extended far inland. A great commercial centre, not least of the slave trade, there could be no more strategic base. Tozer planned to train there an African ministry,[12] and to attack the slave trade at its source.

He and Steere arrived in August 1864 and rented a house from the Sultan, who presented them with five boys taken from an illicit slave dhow (i.e. one which had paid him no duty). One of these, John Swedi, would be the first African admitted to Holy Orders by the Mission. With a fund raised by his theological college of Wells, Tozer bought the Kiungani estate two miles out of town, where the Mission's own theological college would later be built. Next spring fourteen more children, rescued from a slave dhow by the British Navy, were entrusted to Tozer; soon after, his sister and a Miss Jones, the first women workers to reach the Mission, arrived and took charge of them.

In 1866 Tozer's health failed and he went home, leaving Steere in charge. A London barrister and amateur printer who at twenty-six sold his books to feed the poor, Steere had before his ordination tried unsuccessfully to start a religious community. In Lincolnshire he was known as 'a downright shirt-sleeve man and a real Bible parson'.[13] A brilliant linguist, he gave his first five years in Africa to the mastery of Swahili. An earlier CMS missionary, Dr Krapf, had pioneered Biblical translation into a Swahili dialect; by his death in 1882 Steere had nearly completed his own translation of the Bible into the 'mainstream' Swahili of Zanzibar.

In 1867 Alington explored the mountainous Usambala country north of Zanzibar, torn by tribal warfare. A temporary settlement was made in 1868 at Magila, then called Msalabani, 'Place of the Cross': in 1848 Krapf had preached here and carved a cross on a tree-trunk to claim the land for Christ. Seven more years would pass before its permanent settlement, but in 1872 a request to reopen the mission reached Zanzibar. No clergy being available, Steere sent four boys, all under twenty-two: John Swedi, Francis Mabruki (whom Tozer had taken to England for a year[14]), a young English schoolmaster, and Sam Speare, a Suffolk village lad who had met Mabruki in England, joined the Mission at fifteen, and was studying towards ordination. Steere's charge to them summarises UMCA's philosophy of mission:

> You are sent as God's messengers . . . to tell them what He has done for them. If none will receive your message, still God's part has been done, and you will have done yours if you have faithfully declared it. You will not be asked at the last day, How many professing converts have you made? but, Have you faithfully declared the whole counsel of God? . . .
>
> Follow, as far as you can, the customs of the place and people. Quarrel with no one, however much you may be provoked. Treat no one with contempt. Never use violence. . . . Remember in all things the character you bear, and seek to do as Christ would have done in your place. Try to understand the thoughts and difficulties of the people you live amongst. Try to put your message in such words, and deliver it in such a manner, as may make it most intelligible and most acceptable to your hearers . . .
>
> Do not grow weary in well-doing. God is with you; and though you may see no result, your labour is not in vain.[15]

These were years of quiet growth—too quiet, for the Mission was dwindling for lack of recruits. But 'if the staff on earth was small, those who had "fallen on sleep" and were in Paradise were many.'[16] Nothing is more striking than the Mission's vivid sense of fellowship with the Church beyond the veil. In the first thirty years, more than one in three of UMCA's European staff laid down their lives, and at its Jubilee the Mission rejoiced that

> the number of those who have been called from the service of the Mission on earth to bear its needs on their hearts in the more immediate presence of the Lord . . . has in fifty years swelled to more than ninety.[17]

The world's last open slave market stood in Zanzibar. But in May 1872 Stanley published his romantic *How I Found Livingstone* and Livingstone's own horrifying account of the devastation of the interior by Arab slavers. On 20 December, the first Day of Intercession for Mission was observed. Missionary pleas moved the British Government, in January 1873, to negotiate with the Sultan for the suppression of the trade. The Arabs protested the 'blasphemy' of changing a practice as old as Abraham, but when nine men-o'-war appeared off Zanzibar they got the point. With the signing of the treaty on 6 June 1873, the slave market closed for ever.

In September a well-to-do priest recently arrived bought part of the slave market for the Mission; a Hindu merchant gave the site of the whipping-post. Steere began public preaching and discussion there. On Christmas Day 1873, the foundation stone was laid for Christ Church, the Cathedral of Zanzibar. Of this splendid basilica, built of coral and financed by free-will offerings for the purpose (not from Mission funds) Steere himself was master-builder. The altar stands 'exactly where the horrible whipping post once was; and there He who was wounded for our transgressions and by whose stripes we are healed is shewn forth for the sins of the world.'[18]

In February 1874, two of Livingstone's followers, Susi and Chuma, arrived in Zanzibar bearing the embalmed body of their much-loved leader. He had died on his knees in prayer while the treaty ending the slave trade was being negotiated. They buried his heart in Africa, but decided that his bones should lie with *his* ancestors. For nine months they had walked, 1,500 miles from what is now northern Zambia: Livingstone's last journey was an African achievement quite as remarkable as any he planned himself.

England gave Livingstone a State funeral and buried him in Westminster Abbey. More than the man himself (in so many ways a failure) the nation mourned Stanley's idealised image of him. The journals of Livingstone's last years, published in 1874, spoke to Victorian England with the authority of a near-saint. His own confidence in the virtues of the British and their mission to bring Christianity and civilisation to the benighted helped to create and articulate Britain's moral assurance in shouldering the burden of empire. A marked increase in missionary zeal also resulted.

Susi and Chuma returned from Livingstone's funeral to become Steere's right-hand men on all his journeys. These two, baptised after Livingstone's death (Susi thirteen years after), were that archetypal missionary's only permanent converts.

In 1874 Steere was consecrated as Tozer's successor. UMCA had been an 'upper-class' mission whose well-to-do members, or their friends, subsidised the less affluent; no need for stipends had arisen. But Steere had no wealthy friends, and the Mission had shrunk to one priest and five laymen. He tried a new challenge, that

> they who come to the work should either support them-
> selves, or else that, having food and raiment, they should be
> therewith content. £20 a year to such as need it is, in
> addition to their maintenance, the most the Universities'
> Mission offers to those who must also take their lives in
> their hands and forsake (often never to meet again) their
> loved ones at home.[19]

These remained essentially the UMCA terms of service. For most it meant remaining unmarried.

The challenge worked. Steere returned to Zanzibar in 1875 with twenty-one new staff. Among them were William Johnson and Chauncy Maples (of whom we shall hear more), John Farler, a priest who made peace at Magila and built there the Mission's first permanent mainland settlement, and Herbert Woodward, a young layman who, ordained later, was to give fifty-seven years to Africa, thirty of them at Magila. It was at Magila about this time that UMCA realised that a very missionary Islam was also contending for the soul of Africa.

The Mission had established a village for freed slaves at Mbweni in Zanzibar. Steere's mainland trek in 1875 suggested to him that some of them might return to their former homes and plant a Christian village on the way to Lake Nyasa. In 1876 a party of fifty-five set out with two African leaders, William Johnson (a deacon fresh from Oxford, where he had been stroke of the University College eight), a lay superintendent, and Chuma with a caravan of porters. Steere led the way, at first through famine-stricken country. A hundred miles inland they found a land of plenty as Masasi.[20] Here a man welcomed them whom Chuma recognised as a fellow slave freed by Livingstone and Mackenzie. It was a good omen.

> We might seek for years among the forests [the weary settlers said] and never find the exact spot where we were stolen from by the Arabs; here is plenty of water, everything grows well, and war is all but unknown. We are among our own people. Here we will live, and here we will die.[21]

In 1878 Johnson, invalided back to Zanzibar, was replaced by his Oxford friend Chauncy Maples. Another Mbweni party settled at Newala, fifty miles south. In 1879 Johnson returned with John Swedi, now the Mission's first African deacon.[22] All went well until September 1882, when 400 Angoni warriors devastated the area and Masasi was temporarily abandoned.

Meantime Lake Nyasa still beckoned, and late in 1881 Johnson set out, taking with him another Oxford friend, Charles Janson, a young priest of Franciscan simplicity and joy. On 9 February 1882, after a six-week trek, they reached the Mission's original goal. A few days later, alas, Janson died of dysentery. At his lake-side grave, Johnson preached the Resurrection, then went on, alone.

For nearly two years he surveyed the land to which UMCA had first been sent, pondering how it could work in those unhealthy lowlands. His decision fulfilled Mackenzie's last wish: a

Mission steamer to link stations around the 350-mile lake. Johnson hurried home, returning via the Zambesi late in 1884 with the ss *Charles Janson*, broken up into 380 parcels for the sixty-mile portage around the Shiré rapids. Reassembled at the lake, the little steamer ('about the length of a college eight') was launched in September 1885. A safe base was established on Likoma Island, five miles off the eastern shore.

So rapidly did the work grow that in 1892 the diocese of Nyasaland was founded (SPG and SPCK each giving £1,000 toward its endowment). Wilfred Hornby, veteran of six years with the Oxford Mission to Calcutta, which he helped to found, became its first bishop, but ill health soon forced his resignation. Chauncy Maples, now Archdeacon of Likoma, was consecrated to succeed him, but drowned in a storm on the way back: his burial at Nkhotakota on the west shore helped to assure the permanence of the new mission station there.

Nyasaland's third bishop was John Hine, who had attended Livingstone's funeral as a boy, qualified as both doctor and priest, and offered himself to the Mission in 1888.[23] In his time Dr Robert Howard introduced the new preventive use of quinine, whereupon the Mission mortality rate dropped sharply. In 1899 Hine underscored UMCA's stress on indigenisation:

> What this Mission has always professed to aim at is the building-up of a Native Church, which does not mean the baptizing of a number of natives attached to the English Mission, and working under its wing, but the Church of the people of the land, irrespective of European influence, adapting itself to the special circumstances of the race and country.[24]

With twenty lake-side stations, a larger steamer was needed. The 127-foot *Chauncy Maples*, built in Glasgow, was shipped out in 1900 in 3,500 packages for the Shiré portage; her 9½-ton boiler was manhandled sixty-four miles through the hills by 450 Angoni tribesmen. She began work in 1902. Her deck-house was a 'dual-purpose building':

> The schoolroom has seats and desks for 30 students, curtained at the end, shutting off, except at service time, the beautiful altar of teak, inlaid with mother-of-pearl, and

the altar-piece, so dear to sailors, of Christ walking on the water.[25]

'She is our substitute,' said Johnson (who suffered from sea-sickness!)

(1) for railways where there are none; (2) an island in a by no means too peaceful country; (3) a bit of England, where we can live as Englishmen, and work as and with natives . . . (4) a newspaper, a correspondent, and a printing-press in one; (5) last, but not least, a training ground for priests and teachers.[26]

'As she "walks the water" round the Lake', wrote Anderson-Morshead,

carrying all things needful for the spiritual and temporal wants of the Mission, she touches at a station, and a priest is put ashore, while the steamer speeds on to other stations. The priest's visit wakes the station up. Classes and schools are examined and visited. Perhaps some are ready for baptism. A communicants' class is held at night, and the Holy Eucharist celebrated next morning with a reverence and devotion unsurpassed in civilised lands.[27]

In one capacity or another, the 'C.M.' was to serve the Mission for fifty years. She is still on the lake.[28]

In 1883 Charles Alan Smythies (whose enthusiasm had already built an iron mission hut in Cardiff into St German's, Roath) succeeded Steere as Bishop of the Mission. Next year the long-planned theological college at Kiungani was begun, for

it is always better, if possible, to educate the native clergy in Africa than in England . . . where the good of their education is balanced by loss of touch with their own people, and by an acquired taste for luxuries not easily obtainable and not desirable in a poor church.[29]

An indefatigable traveller, on his second visit to Magila (in 1885) Smythies took part in a notable demonstration. Nine miles north stands Mlinga, 'spirit mountain' of the ancestors of the Bondei. It was death for any mortal to ascend it . . . until one market day, in full view of the people, Smythies and Herbert Woodward, now Archdeacon of Magila, boldly climbed Mlinga—and returned. A cross was planted on top, 'as a sign that the God of the spirits of all flesh had taken possession of Mlinga.'[30] The spirits were conquered on Likoma, too: in 1903 the foundation-stone of St Peter's Cathedral was laid near the spot where formerly witches were burnt. Dedicated in 1905, Likoma Cathedral is still the largest church in Africa, though the effective centre of the diocese, now called 'Lake Malawi', has shifted to Nkhotakota.

The European scramble for colonies was on. Smythies needed all his very considerable statesmanship as the Mission's work was divided into three 'spheres of influence': Likoma, Nkhotakota and the southern end of the lake were British, as was Zanzibar; the east shore was Portuguese; the rest of the mainland work, German.

> Like Broughton in Australia, Gray in Cape Town
>> saw the Church in the light newly thrown by the Tractarians, as the creation of God, not of the State. Like Selwyn in New Zealand, Gray in South Africa set himself to build up the Church almost from nothing, on principles drawn from the study of its early history.[31]

In 1857 Gray held a synod to discuss a diocesan constitution. A small minority did not want a self-governing Church *of* South Africa, but 'the Church of *England in* South Africa'—subject to the Crown.[32] The issue went to the Privy Council, which in 1863 declared that Gray's Letters Patent had no force in South Africa, which now had its own legislature. A similar judgement was made in 1865 in the Colenso controversy.[33] These defeats of Gray's *legal* authority actually strengthened his case for the Church's freedom to order its life by its own *spiritual authority*—the indispensable prerequisite for self-governing Anglican provinces. The importance of the issues involved led the Canadian Church in 1867—the year when the British North America Act made Canada the first self-governing dominion of the British Commonwealth—to ask for the first Lambeth Conference. The Anglican Communion had begun its family consultations.

Also in 1867 the Second Reform Bill gave the vote to the British working classes—apparently unnoticed by Karl Marx in the Reading Room of the British Museum, who that year published the first volume of *Das Kapital*. In South Africa, diamonds were found near the Orange River.

With UMCA's Tozer was consecrated in 1863 Edward Twells for 'Bloemfontein'[34]—beyond the Orange River and the Drakensberg, but with no other boundaries. Twells could persuade no other clergy to join him. He stiffened his demands:

> Let us put before them the hard life of a missionary brotherhood. This may attract those who are able to devote their whole lives to our Lord, and who will not be attracted by settled income and easy living.[35]

Thus was born the Society of St Augustine, the first Anglican religious community overseas.[36] Its members, living in poverty and obedience, were to be trained for ordination. The first six men sailed in July 1867 with their superior, Canon Beckett, but war delayed until 1869 their reaching the farms Twells had bought for them at Modderpoort on the Basutoland border. Their first home was a cave, with

> a room 12 ft. by 14 ft. for a chapel, besides a small sleeping room screened off by a large detached stone. Both rooms are much improved by digging away the floors, so that I can now stand upright in the chapel and sit upright in the bedroom.[37]

Modderpoort became a centre for European and African work, language study and translation, and mission into Basutoland, a British protectorate since 1868. It remains a powerhouse of prayer for the diocese, with the cave chapel a great place of pilgrimage.

Anglican work in Zululand was begun (by Colenso with SPG help) at KwaMagwaza in 1860. In 1870 a bishopric was endowed in memory of Mackenzie. The Zulu wars of the late 1870s destroyed KwaMagwaza; in 1881 a new diocesan centre near the battlefield of Isandhlwana was established as a memorial. Charles and Margaret Johnson now began, at St Augustine's near Rorke's Drift, forty-six years of building up a missionary parish with thirty-seven outstations. The great parish church was built in 1898, with the help of £1,000 from SPG—

> a real central church, large enough to allow the people from

the little out-stations in the district to congregate together at this centre on all great festivals, to teach them that they are all members of the one parish church.[38]

Henry Callaway, a priest-doctor, pioneered medical work at Springvale in Zululand. In 1873 he became first bishop of the diocese of St John's, 'Kaffraria' (the Transkei), founded[39] by the Episcopal Church of Scotland, which had just set up its own Mission Board. Callaway planted a strategic centre at Umtata, where three tribal areas meet. Today St John's has five diocesan hospitals—more than any other diocese in the Anglican Communion. In recent years the South African Government has given generous financial support to African hospitals, but whether or how long this will continue in the new 'Bantustans', of which the Transkei is the first, remains to be seen.

In the 1850s the frontier forts along the Kei River were replaced with mission stations—Grahamstown's 'four Evangelists': St Luke's at Umhalla's, St John's at Sandili's, St Matthew's at Keiskama Hoek, St Mark's at Kreli's. By 1881 Grahamstown's clergy had increased from six to forty-seven and its bishop could write that

> whereas 25 years ago we had not a single Kafir convert, we are now counting our communicants by thousands; that we have a Native ministry growing up; and that the foundation is laid of a Native ministry fund supported entirely by themselves.

And this had been achieved 'mainly through the continuous stream of bounty derived from the SPG.'[40]

The area between the Limpopo River boundary of white settlement and the Zambesi was ruled by the Matabele. In 1876 William Greenstock, SPG missionary in Grahamstown for twenty years, asked Society help for a trek to Bulawayo. Lobengula, the Matabele chief, hoping for British protection from Boer threats to his land, granted Greenstock's request to plant a mission. SPG backed the plan, but the first Boer war intervened.

In 1888 Cecil Rhodes, dreaming of a British Empire spreading civilisation along a Cape-to-Cairo railway, obtained from Lobengula a concession to dig for gold, and in 1889 a Royal Charter for his British South Africa Company. On 12 September

1890 an expedition of 200 European settlers, 500 police, 150 African labourers and two chaplains founded Salisbury in Mashonaland.

Bishop Knight-Bruce of Bloemfontein had already planned a Mashonaland mission, with a promise from SPG of £7,000 for the first seven years. In 1891 he became first bishop of Mashonaland (including all of modern Rhodesia), with his headquarters at Umtali. With him came five European lay missionaries and five African catechists. Among the latter was a gifted evangelist and translator, Bernard Mizeki, born in Portuguese territory and educated in Cape Town.

In 1893, after a brief war, Lobengula was driven from Bulawayo and the Company took over. White settlement increased, and the Church spread among both Matabele and Shona. But a second war broke out, and on 18 June 1896 Mizeki was murdered. His grave has become a shrine which attracts many thousands of pilgrims each year on the anniversary of his martyrdom.

In 1898 St Augustine's, Penhalonga was begun with SPG help as an industrial training centre at Umtali, by a little Mashonaland Missionary Brotherhood. Reinforced by Mirfield Fathers in 1915 and Grahamstown Sisters in 1919, Penhalonga remains a spiritual powerhouse to this day.

Company rule in Rhodesia lasted until 1923, when the white minority were granted a large measure of self-government as a Crown colony. In 1923 the world thought it perfectly natural that a handful of Europeans (33,260 in the 1921 census) should rule half a million Africans.

CHAPTER SIX

The Ancient East

The heart of India—Missionary brotherhoods
The first independent Asian Church
Christianity and commerce—Of priests and prayer

IN AMERICA, the Caribbean and Africa, missionary encounter with alien cultures was mostly with preliterate primal societies; Zanzibar's Muslim Arabs had proved impervious to the Gospel. The see cities around the edge of India—Calcutta and Madras (both founded by the East India Company) and Bombay—were in 1851 as much British as Indian, and 'John Company' preferred the Church to remain the British garrison at prayer. Its spread up the Ganges valley was mainly the work of CMS, though from 1833 SPG worked in Cawnpore.[1] Apart from Bishop's College, missionary contact with the 'heathen' in North India had been mainly with illiterate folk of village and bazaar.[2]

Very different was the encounter at Delhi in the heart of India, centre both of a sophisticated Hindu civilisation thousands of years old and of the Muslim Moghul empire which had dominated India since 1192. In Delhi, British-controlled since 1802, the garrison church of St James was built in 1836. Its congregation formed a missionary association and collected funds, but until the arrival of M.J. Jennings as chaplain in 1851, the only evangelism in Delhi was by a solitary Baptist preacher in the bazaars.

Ram Chandra, Professor of Higher Mathematics at the Government College, was a high-caste Hindu. Western education had destroyed his Hindu faith, though he believed vaguely in one

God. He respected the British, but surely they could not really believe in Christianity, since they did not bother to teach it?[3] One Sunday he took a curious student to Evensong at St James's and saw there some English gentlemen whom he knew to be educated and enlightened, 'and many of them kneeled down and appeared to be praying most devoutly.'[4] Deeply moved by the Establishment at prayer, he went home, got out his Bible, and began to pray to God to make him a Christian. On 11 July 1852, with his friend Chimmam Lal, Assistant Surgeon at the Delhi Hospital, Ram Chandra asked for Baptism.

A tremendous stir was caused: 'It was like God giving these men to our faith and prayers,' wrote Jennings, who at once asked SPG to send missionaries. The Society endowed the Mission with £8,000 from its Jubilee Fund (£1,500 had been collected in Delhi), and in 1854 sent two priests, Stuart Jackson and A.R. Hubbard. The Bishop of Madras visited Delhi in 1856 and thought it 'among the most hopeful and promising of our Indian mission fields.' Twelve converts were confirmed in March 1857.

But the Delhi Church was to be baptized in blood. On 11 May 1857 the Indian garrison mutinied, killed every European in Delhi and every Indian Christian save one; Ram Chandra, hidden by his family, alone escaped. Cawnpore, too, was devastated. When the news reached England, SPG declared that 'although the Delhi Mission, so blessed of God in its commencement, seems to be annihilated, the Society is resolved—God being its helper—to plant again the Cross of Christ in that city.'[5]

An appeal for funds and workers raised £19,000, and Thomas Skelton, a Fellow of Jesus College, Cambridge, volunteered. Arriving in Delhi early in 1859, he found a flourishing school already opened by Ram Chandra. More high-caste converts were asking for baptism: Tara Chand, ordained in 1863, was to be an SPG missionary for nearly fifty years. In 1860 Robert and Priscilla Winter arrived, through whose devoted labours the Mission was to expand greatly. Robert founded schools, preached in the bazaars, toured nearby villages. Mrs Winter, a doctor's daughter with some medical knowledge of her own, began visiting the zenanas—the secluded women's quarters where Muslim and Hindu wives led narrowly restricted lives. When Skelton was called to Calcutta in 1863 as Principal of Bishop's College, the Winters took charge.

In 1867 St Stephen's Church was dedicated in memory of the Delhi martyrs. The same year the SPG Ladies' Association (started in 1866) began supporting women missionaries in Delhi schools and zenana visiting. In 1870 Priscilla Winter started a dispensary: out of her zenana medical work was to grow St Stephen's Hospital for women, opened in 1881 as a memorial to her. Its nursing superintendent from 1908-38, Alice Wilkinson, pioneered the establishment of nursing standards in India, culminating in 1947 in the All-India Nursing Council. In 1974 St Stephen's Hospital began building on land next door, to double its size and become a general hospital.

One of the most important results of the Tractarian movement was the revival of the religious life. India has its own indigenous form of religious community in the Hindu *ashram*. Early Jesuit missionaries adopted the dress and manner of the Hindu *sannyasi* or 'holy man'. Anglican religious life came to India in 1874 with the Cowley Fathers in Bombay. Three years later, with SPG and SPCK help, the Wantage Sisters were established at Poona. (SPG had already in 1868 begun work east of Bombay in the Ahmednagar area, where large numbers of outcastes were becoming Christian.)

In 1877 Queen Victoria was proclaimed Empress of India, and the diocese of Lahore was established, including Delhi and the Punjab. Its first bishop was Thomas French, twenty-four years a devoted CMS missionary at Agra, then rector of St Ebbe's, Oxford. In 1876 he and Brooke Foss Westcott of Cambridge had both become convinced that the universities were 'providentially fitted to train men who shall interpret the faith of the West to the East, and bring back to us new illustrations of the one infinite and eternal Gospel.'[6] Westcott later surmised that 'the final commentary on St John's Gospel will be written by an Indian.' He himself gave four sons to India.

Edward Bickersteth,[7] Fellow of Pembroke College, Cambridge, and greatly influenced by both French and Westcott, now proposed a missionary brotherhood for India. CMS felt unable to back a venture whose members it could not choose; SPG gladly shared its support from the start. In 1877 Bickersteth and J.D.M. Murray sailed as the first members of the Cambridge Mission to Delhi (CMD), followed soon by four others. Though he headed the Mission for only five years, Bickersteth's spiritual influence was enormous.

The Government College in Delhi had just closed; Winter, hoping the Cambridge Mission might fill the gap, at once handed over St Stephen's High School with its 500 boys. A college department was opened which in 1882 became a constituent body of the new Punjab University. The influence of St Stephen's College on educated Indians of all faiths or none has been incalculable; USPG still supports one of its staff members. At the other end of the social scale, the CMD worked among the *chamars*, low-caste leather workers in the city, and in the surrounding villages.

The Cambridge Brotherhood take no life vows, but live a common life of prayer and work under a rule. On it have been modelled many other missionary brotherhoods, in India and elsewhere. In 1944 it changed its name to the Brotherhood of the Ascended Christ, and its rule so as to withdraw from institutional and organisational work and be more fully a body 'with prayer as its first work'. Priscilla Winter's women workers had since 1871 lived together under a rule in St Stephen's Home, and in 1886 became St Stephen's Community—still supported, like the Brotherhood, by USPG.

Bishop Edward Johnson of Calcutta, seeing the need for work among Calcutta University students, appealed to his own university for a mission of the CMD sort. The result, in 1880, was the Oxford Mission to Calcutta (OMC), which also took over work in the Ganges Delta. Johnson re-established Bishop's College as a theological college, and in 1890 its Principal, Henry Whitehead, became also Superior of the OMC. This brought the OMC and SPG into a close association which still continues. Today the Oxford Mission (which since 1900 includes a Sisterhood) works also in Bangladesh.

The diocese of Chota Nagpur was founded among aboriginal hill tribes driven from the plains by invading Indo-Aryans five centuries before Christ. Mission among them was begun in 1845 by Johannes Gossner, a German Lutheran. On his initiative, most of his converts later asked Bishop Milman of Calcutta to receive them into the English Church. In 1869, with due inquiry and SPG's agreement to take over, Milman received 7,000 of them, confirmed their communicants and ordained their pastors to the priesthood. Centred on Ranchi, this became one of SPG's largest Indian commitments.

In 1890 SPG raised the endowment for the diocese, whose bishop at once appealed for more clergy. At that very moment the Society received from five students of Trinity College, Dublin, an offer to serve as a community (on the pattern of CMD and OMC) anywhere in the world. In 1891 SPG sent the Dublin University Mission to open new work at Hazaribagh, sixty miles north of Ranchi. Jointly supported by the university and by USPG, the DUM is still at work.

As at Delhi, the Church in Cawnpore rose again after the Mutiny, but by 1889 its staff had shrunk to a single Indian priest. The Bishop of Calcutta appealed to SPG. In the same post came a letter from Westcott (now Canon of Westminster) saying two of his sons wished to offer themselves, preferably for India. George and Foss Westcott brought new life to the Church in the great industrial city of Cawnpore. In 1895 George asked SPG to let them form a brotherhood. The Society provided two more stipends and enlarged their house; in 1896 two more priests joined them. The Cawnpore Brotherhood continued its work, specialising in industrial training, until the Second World War.

The Day of Intercession for mission had an immense impact. 1873 saw not only the end of the East African slave trade, but also the suspension of Japan's edicts against Christianity and the arrival in Tokyo of two SPG missionaries.

Jesuits had planted a flourishing Church in Japan in the sixteenth century, but fierce persecution early in the seventeenth wiped it out. Japan remained closed to foreigners until an American gunboat sailed into Tokyo harbour in 1854. American missionaries of all sorts soon followed. A Russian Orthodox missionary started a flourishing Japanese Orthodox Church.

French Roman Catholics at Nagasaki in 1865 were astounded to be greeted by several thousand 'crypto-Christians' who had handed down their traditions secretly for 250 years. CMS sent six missionaries.

The 1872 Day of Intercession brought SPG both gifts for work in Japan and offers of service. Two priests were chosen, Alexander Shaw (a Canadian, first overseas missionary of his Church) and William Wright. Late in 1873 they settled into a disued Buddist temple in Tokyo and began learning Japanese. Their first convert was baptised a year later. In 1876 SPG sent two missionaries to the great seaport of Kobe, where a boys' school was opened in 1878, and one for girls, the Shoin Jo Gakko, in 1889. The same year the Emperor granted a constitution giving Japan the forms of representative government, though real power remained in military hands until 1945.

Bickersteth, invalided home from Delhi, was about to return there when in 1886 he was called to Japan as a bishop, to help CMS, SPG and American Episcopal missions grow into a Church. It was imperative that they do so quickly. Japan was adopting Western ways with astonishing speed and efficiency, including some of the less attractive aspects of nationalism. The Church, drawn mostly from the professional classes, was urban, educated and ready for self-government.

Within a year of Bickersteth's arrival, constitution and canons were drafted and the Nippon Sei Ko Kai (Japan Holy Catholic Church) held its first synod. The same year Bickersteth founded in Tokyo the Brotherhood of St Andrew,[8] along CMD lines, and the parallel St Hilda's Mission for women. Both worked among the very large numbers of Japanese eager for Western education. The chief means of evangelisation in Japan have been Christian education (at every level from kindergarten to university) and the Japanese desire to learn English from a native speaker.

Nowhere did the 1872 Day of Intercession bear such fruit as at St Peter's, Eaton Square (London), whose vicar had originated the idea in the SPG Standing Committee. His own curate, Charles Perry Scott, offered himself. One of the congregation offered

SPG £500 a year for five years for a mission in China. Miles Greenwood, curate of Padiham in Lancashire, volunteered the same day, and after some language and medical studies the two left for North China in 1874. The St Peter's Missionary Guild backed them with prayer and money and grew into the North China & Shantung Missionary Association. In 1880 the same anonymous donor endowed the North China bishopric with £10,000.[9] Scott, whose leadership had been demonstrated in SPG's relief efforts in the 1878 famine (in which more than nine million perished), was consecrated its first bishop.

China's is the world's oldest continuous civilisation and, except for Buddhism from India, its culture is wholly indigenous. The Confucianism of its traditional high culture is a system for regulating society through ethics, ceremonial, and respect for ancestors: Confucian orthodoxy, like Marxism, regards religion as the opiate of the people. At the opposite pole is Taoism, originally a philosophical 'way of the universe' free of man-made restraints, but blended with magic and spirit-worship into a folk religion. The civilisations of Korea, Japan and South East Asia derive from China's, and she knew no others. Behind her Great Wall, built against barbarian invaders in 214 B.C., the 'Middle Kingdom' *was* civilisation; beyond her orbit were only 'foreign devils'.

Nestorian Christianity and Islam reached China in the seventh century; Venetian traders and Franciscan missionaries in the thirteenth, Portuguese traders and Jesuit missionaries in the sixteenth. The Jesuits settled in Peking, commending themselves to the scholarly upper classes by their scientific knowledge. By 1701 there were 300,000 Chinese Christians. The first Protestant missionary, Robert Morrison of the LMS, arrived in Canton in 1807 and spent twenty-seven years translating the Bible into Chinese.

Nowhere has the partnership of Christianity and commerce been so ambivalent as in China. Throughout the Manchu Dynasty (1644-1911) Western pressure steadily increased. Chinese silks and cottons, teas and porcelains were prized in Europe and paid for largely with gold and silver, for China saw no need of anything the Western barbarians had to offer. To reverse this adverse balance of trade, the opium trade was begun, mainly from India and in British ships—a commerce quite as soul-destroying as the slave trade. CMS protested that 'our whole course upon the coast of China has been one of injustice . . . We are the great opium producers, the great poison-vendors of the East.'[10] China's understandable efforts to stop this drug traffic, and British insistence on continuing it, led to the Opium Wars.

We may have forgotten the humiliating 'Unequal Treaties'; China has not. In 1842 Hong Kong was ceded to Britain and five treaty ports were forced open to Western trade in opium and the mass-produced goods which ruined China's rural industries. CMS began work in Shanghai: its work in China was much more extensive than SPG's. American missionaries of every sort were more numerous still. SPG and the Colonial Bishoprics' Fund in 1849 endowed the diocese of Victoria (Hong Kong), with spiritual oversight of consular and trading stations in China. The same year SPG helped found St Paul's College in Hong Kong and in 1861 sent Edward Venn to found schools in Singapore.

In 1858 the interior of China was opened to Christian mission. Two years later William (later Bishop) Russell observed that

> by the Treaty now ratified, the whole of China is opened up to the preaching of the Gospel: but while we recognise in it the Hand of God, we recognise at the same time the hand of man, cruel, covetous, Godless man. By the very instrument by which China is declared to have thrown open her gate to the free and unrestricted preaching of the Gospel, it is equally declared that she has been forced by Christian England to throw open her gate to the free and unrestricted introduction of opium.[11]

Such was the situation when, after an abortive attempt in Peking in 1863, SPG's work in North China began with the arrival of Scott and Greenwood.

Christianity came to Korea from China in the eighteenth century, but until the late nineteenth century Christians were bitterly persecuted. Native Korean religion is a shamanism like that of Siberia to the north, mixed with spirit-worship and sorcery; Confucianism and Chinese Buddhism are also very influential. Korea's neighbours have always coveted her natural resources: China long regarded her as a vassal; Japan tried unsuccessfully to conquer her in the sixteenth century; in 1876 Western-style gunboat diplomacy forced Korea open to Japanese trade. The West soon followed.

In 1887 Scott of North China and Bickersteth of Japan visited Korea and strongly urged a mission there. As missionary bishop, the Archbishop of Canterbury consecrated Charles Corfe, a much-loved naval chaplain and a dedicated and ascetic Catholic, with missionary experience in North China. SPG gave Corfe £500 a year (soon raised to £1,500). It was a forbidding task—'like attacking a battleship with a dinghy', said Corfe. The Archbishop 'told me that he had no pay to offer, that the ground was yet untrodden by English missionaries, that he had no one to give me for a companion, and that the country was unsettled and hostile to Christianity'.[12]

Corfe also needed priests and prayer. He wanted a Korean Missionary Brotherhood who, like himself, would serve without pay beyond bare maintenance. He asked for five priests; one responded, and a dozen laymen. The priest was Herbert Kelly—son of an Evangelical Lancashire parsonage, deeply influenced at Oxford by the Catholicism of Kingsley and Maurice, who shared Corfe's views on mission. He was told to stay home and train the laymen. Such was the origin of the Society of the Sacred Mission (SSM). Herbert Woodward, home on furlough from UMCA in 1893, was professed with Kelly and together they constituted the Great Chapter which drafted the first SSM constitution. Thus began the long relationship between UMCA and SSM, which had a priory at Mkuzi (near Magila) from 1913 to 1929 and again in the 1940s and '50s. In 1902-3, the year of their move to Kelham, the SSM took over and expanded the Modderpoort mission in Bloemfontein and what is now Lesotho, a work they still continue. Woodward himself, transferred to Modderpoort in 1920, later returned to lay his bones in Zanzibar in 1932.

At home, Corfe founded an Association for Prayer and Work, with a regular intercession leaflet (edited by G.R. Bullock Webster) and *Morning Calm*, a periodical still published by the Korean Mission. Meantime, some keen young London clergy formed in 1891 a Junior Clergy Missionary Association (JCMA) 'in connection with the SPG' for 'deepening and developing the missionary spirit' in themselves and their parishes through study and prayer—a forerunner of the SPG Association of Missionary Candidates. By 1900 there were seventy-seven local JMCAs with nearly 4,000 members; by 1908 nearly 400 had gone overseas, some with SPG, others to serve among English settlers in Canada, Australia and South Africa.

In 1895 the JCMA began a quarterly intercession paper, which Bullock Webster took over in 1900 and combined with the Korean one. Such was the origin of the *Quarterly Intercession Paper* (*QIP*), now used by more than 16,000 people all over the world. Entrusted to SPG in 1931, it is independently edited and covers a wide range of missionary concerns.

The vast, sparsely populated Australian outback has always posed pastoral problems. In 1897 the Bishop of Rockhampton, urgently needing clergy, went to see B.F. Westcott, now Bishop of Durham. Thirty members of the Durham JCMA had just asked Westcott's direction with regard to overseas service. The St Andrew's Bush Brotherhood, posted at Longreach in 1897, was the first of many such brotherhoods in Australia, living and working for a period under a rule and caring for the isolated folk of the outback.[13] The Society never made grants to Bush Brotherhoods, but still publicises their work and helps to find, train and send recruits.

THE TWENTIETH CENTURY:

'Ye are witnesses' (Luke 24.48)

CHAPTER SEVEN

Mission in the Decline of the West

The end of an era—A twentieth-century SPG
Medical mission—A twentieth-century UMCA
New nationalisms and old—The death of Christendom
Indigenisation—Urban mission—The ecumenical
movement—The home front
between the wars—The end of a world

IN 1897 BRITAIN celebrated its Queen Empress's Diamond Jubilee, but the twilight of empire had already begun. In the missionary exuberance of 1819 Reginald Heber could write

Can we, whose souls are lighted
With wisdom from on high,
Can we to men benighted
The lamp of life deny?

Livingstone believed fervently in the mission of empire itself. But in 1897 Kipling cast his 'Recessional' in the form of a prayer for mercy, writing of a heathen heart that was not on Greenland's icy mountains nor India's coral strand but in England, putting her trust in the 'reeking tube and iron shard' of the European arms race. How members of an apostate society can be messengers of the Gospel was to be *the* missionary problem of the West in the twentieth century. It took quite a while for the penny to drop.

In the year that Queen Victoria died, SPG kept its bicentenary —marked, among other things, by a pamphlet significantly entitled *The Spiritual Expansion of the Empire* and by Charles Pascoe's monumental *Two Hundred Years of SPG*. Since its third

Jubilee, four overseas Anglican provinces had been born and four Lambeth conferences held. In 1901 SPG supported 939 overseas missionaries and 11,000 parishes supported it; its income reached £206,799. On the Continent it provided thirty-two permanent and 104 seasonal chaplaincies and held forty churches in trust.

Two able Secretaries had followed the great Hawkins. William Bullock, scholarly curate of St Anne's, Soho, learnt the trade in a fourteen-year apprenticeship to Hawkins, whom he succeeded in 1864, appointing Henry Tucker as his own assistant. 'Dear Bullock,' wrote UMCA's Mackenzie on his way to consecration and death,

> I do not know if you twine yourself into the affections of all the missionaries you see before they leave England . . . You live in my memory associated with so many words and acts of sympathy that I shall not soon lose the picture of you in my mind.[1]

It was Bullock who started daily prayers in the Society head-quarters. In 1865, in response to parish demands, 'real mission-aries' on furlough began to undertake deputations. In 1866 the Ladies' Association[2] began supporting women missionaries. In 1869 SPG joined in urging Convocation to promote mission as an essential work of the Church, and Diocesan Boards of Missions began to be formed.

Tucker took over in 1879, with a beard like an Old Testament patriarch and a character to match.[3] A diligent overseas corre-spondent, he also greatly strengthened the home front. Financial support of mission was shifting from the wealthy few to countless ordinary folk at the grassroots. Country members protested that SPG business was conducted almost wholly by London members; in 1882 a Supplementary Charter from Queen Victoria gave executive power to the Standing Committee, each diocese now having a representative.[4] Children's work was begun indepen-dently by the Ladies' Association in 1891 and the Worcester JCMA in 1896; in 1897 these efforts merged into the King's Messengers, which by 1900 had 500 branches.

In 1896 SPG received from the will of Alfred Marriott £71,325 to be spent within six years for overseas churches, hospitals and colleges: by 1900, 331 churches and twenty hospitals had been built and eighty colleges aided; the income from a further £111,230 of the Marriott Bequest still helps overseas Churches today.

In 1901 SPG called as Secretary the first of a long line of missionary bishops, Henry Montgomery of Tasmania—a man of prayer, vision and an administrative genius inherited by his son 'Monty', the World War II field marshal. 'Is it episcopal vocation?' cabled the startled bishop; 'World-wide oversight surely eipscopal,' came the reply.[5] Montgomery, who found a dedicated and diligent staff in an office without telephone or typewriter, soon brought the Society's somewhat dusty structure into the twentieth century.

In 1902 he appointed full-time Home and Editorial Secretaries. In 1903 the Publications Department was organised and a serious and successful quarterly review of missionary problems, *The East and the West*, launched.[6] In 1904 the Women's Missionary Association (hitherto an independent body) became a Committee for Women's Work within SPG, and a training hostel for women missionaries was opened in Wandsworth.

Pressed by the JCMA, the Society in 1904 opened a fund for missionary candidates unable to finance their own ordination training, with a Candidates' Committee to administer it. The next year a Braille Department of volunteers began transcribing missionary literature for the blind.[7] Mary Jane Hutchings, a blind and deaf pauper in a Devonshire workhouse, read the new Braille *QIP* and sent to the Candidates' Fund five shillings saved out of friends' gifts to her. Reporting this 'widow's mite', the *QIP* invited other five-shilling gifts. The Candidates' Five Shilling Fund has raised so far over £300,000 and still provides a substantial proportion (£6,000 in 1973) of the money available to USPG for missionary training.

SPG's headquarters at 19 Delahay Street was bursting at the seams when the site was requisitioned for Government offices. The Society's present home at 15 Tufton Street (hard by Church House and Westminster Abbey) is strategically located, in the Establishment but not of it, and easily accessible. Its foundation-stone laid in 1907, SPG House was completed within a year at a cost of £36,700. £9,385 came from gifts, including £750 from the American Church for Chapel and Board Room panelling, the rest from the sale of the old house.

When the cupboards were turned out at 19 Delahay Street, there came to light the dusty remains of White Kennett's *Americana* collection, given to SPG in 1713. In 1917 these were examined, found to be now of antiquarian rather than missionary value, and offered to the British Museum, which kept eighty items of which not even it had copies. The rest, sold at Sotheby's, fetched £4,140. Through the income from this, one SPG founder-member still helps what has become probably the most comprehensive and up-to-date missionary library in the country, with over 25,000 volumes.

Some old missions were reopened in these years. In 1904 SPG was asked to resume work on the West African 'Gold Coast', where since 1824 the Anglican Church had been represented only by chaplains. When the diocese of Accra was founded in 1909, the Society provided the bishop's stipend.

Around the turn of the century Codrington went through another bad patch, from which SPG rescued it with grants from its Bicentenary Fund and the Marriott Bequest. At the Codrington bicentenary in 1910 it was noted that 'the College has given to the West Indies not only bishops and the bulk of the clergy, but chief justices, physicians, planters and men of leading position.'[8] English ordinands intending to work in the Caribbean began training there. Training colleges for men and women teachers were opened in 1913 and 1914, and in 1915, Codrington Girls' High School.

In 1906 Montgomery visited Canada (whose SPG grants had ended in 1900) and came back convinced of new need to help the Church there to cope with the flood of immigrants to the prairies. The Archbishops of Canterbury and York were like-minded, and in 1910 SPG suspended its own appeal in order to back and provide an office for the Archbishops' Western Canada Fund. Groups of missionaries were to work on bush brotherhood lines, for their keep and £2 a month pocket-money. Three such groups were sent, twenty-eight clergy and twenty-four laymen in all, plus three nurses and four other women workers. In 1920 one of the Fund's area secretaries, Eva Hasell, founded the Western Canada Sunday School Caravan Mission and 'Sunday School by Post', which at its peak served the pioneer settlers of seven Canadian provinces.

Randall Davidson, Montgomery's school-fellow at Harrow, had been connected with SPG for twenty years when he became Archbishop of Canterbury in 1903.[9] No other archbishop ever cared so deeply about mission or so identified himself personally with 'my Society'. He made Montgomery a secretary of the 1908 Lambeth Conference; Montgomery himself planned the preceding eight-day Pan-Anglican Congress which did more than anything else to make the Anglican Communion conscious of itself as such and raised a £350,000 thank-offering for Christian education overseas. 1908 also saw the first SPG Royal Albert Hall rally, and the start of the annual *SPG Cycle of Prayer and Praise*, listing all missionaries by name.

UMCA, called into being by a doctor, saw healing as part of its task from the start. SPG sent out the first of many priest-doctors in 1713, but it was two centuries before Codrington's vision of mission to the whole man became fully respectable. SPG first deliberately planned medical mission as such in South India in 1854. At Sawyerpur in Tinnevelly it introduced medical evangelists—Indian laymen with simple medical training. European missionaries with medical knowledge also opened dispensaries for treatment of simple ailments: one of these, John Strachan, SPG sent for full medical training. St Luke's Hospital, started by Strachan at Nazareth, a Christian village founded by converts, was so successful that others followed, both in India and, when Strachan became Bishop of Rangoon in 1882, in Burma. SPG also began medical work in North China and Korea.

Many supporters hesitated about medicine and nursing: were they 'real missionary work' in the same sense as education? But in 1907 the first SPG summer school asked the Society to organise its medical work properly. In 1908 a Medical Missions Committee was formed, in 1909 the first Medical Missions Secretary was appointed, and in 1911 the Medical Missions Department was set up, with its own fund. The next two decades saw enormous expansion of medical work by both SPG and UMCA, based on hospitals ranging from those like St Stephen's, Delhi, to the one UMCA built at Korogwe in 1911 for £5 'to replace one that had fallen down in a thunderstorm'![10]

UMCA kept two Jubilees: that of Livingstone's appeal at Cambridge in 1907, and that of the founding of the Mission at Oxford in 1909. At the first, the Mission resolved to press westward from Nyasaland; the second announced the redoubtable Dr Hine's acceptance of the new bishopric of Northern Rhodesia. In 1910 he set off on foot with three companions to plan the evangelisation of an area twice the size of the British Isles. Hine walked 2,500 miles that year. In that land of many languages four mission stations were eventually planted: Mapanza in the south and Msoro in the east (1911), Chipili in the north (1914), Fiwila in the centre (1924).

Meanwhile the home organisation was growing. The Mission had no office of its own until 1882, when it moved out of SPG into nearby 14 Delahay Street. The following year *Central Africa*, the chief UMCA periodical, began to appear. In 1889 Duncan Travers came home from Magila to begin thirty-six years as UMCA General Secretary. Children's work began in 1890 with the formation of the Coral League. In 1897 the office moved to roomier quarters at 9 Dartmouth Street. In 1903 the League of Associates began its support of UMCA. Mary Anderson-Morshead's *History of the UMCA* inspired new efforts with its thrilling account of the first half-century.

In 1898 a twenty-seven-year-old curate of St Matthew's, Westminster, sailed for Zanzibar to become the most colourful and influential personality in UMCA history: Frank Weston. Greatly concerned for indigenisation and local training of priests, he planned and built up St Mark's Theological College at Mazizini. In 1908 he succeeded Hine as Bishop of Zanzibar. UMCA had always been Tractarian ('Prayer Book Catholic'); Weston's Anglo-Catholicism now set its stamp on the Mission, especially in Zanzibar and Masasi. No empty ritualism, this was rooted in a profoundly Evangelical personal devotion to Christ.

Weston charged his staff:

> Our first work is to make over to the African Church the heritage of the consecrated Christian character. It is at once our privilege to proclaim the good news of the divine life brought to us by and in our Saviour, and our duty to display that life in action within our society . . . Prayer is the only known way of bringing to our heathen people the power that is to make them Christian and to bring them to heaven.[11]

Every priest was directed to give two hours to God in prayer each morning, every lay missionary asked to give one hour.

Though a passionate controversialist in defence of 'Catholic principles', Weston longed for the reunion of Christendom and was one of the chief architects of the 1920 Lambeth 'Appeal to All Christian People'. He was also the hero of the Anglo-Catholic Congresses of 1920 and 1923. At the latter Weston urged:

> You have your Mass, you have your altars, you have begun to get your tabernacles. Now go out into the highways and hedges, and look for Jesus in the ragged and the naked, in the oppressed and the sweated, in those who have lost hope and in those who are struggling to make good. Look for Jesus in them; and, when you find him, gird yourselves with his towel of fellowship and wash his feet in the person of his brethren.[12]

Perhaps Weston's finest achievement was founding the Community of the Sacred Passion (CSP). 1911 saw the first professions, and the Community grew steadily. The first African novice was clothed in 1928: she did not stay, but it started many thinking. Thirteen years later the first novices were clothed in the African *Chama cha Mariamu Mtakatifu* (Community of St Mary), which goes from strength to strength today.

In 1910-11 Montgomery toured the Far East, where Japan was collecting colonies in the Western manner. The Sino-Japanese War of 1894-5 had detached Korea from China's orbit. In Formosa, which became a Japanese colony, the Nippon Sei Ko Kai at once began work which SPG later helped. In 1905 Japan had astounded the world by defeating Russia and annexing Korea. The decline of the West had begun, and a new sun was rising in the East.

Already in 1904 Montgomery had seen that a Christian Japan could 'revolutionise Asia and refresh the faith of the West',[13] Top priority was training Japanese priests. £30,000 from the Pan-Anglican Thank-offering Fund helped establish in 1911 a Central Theological College into which SPG and CMS merged their own colleges. Herbert Kelly of Kelham, on the College staff 1913-19, perceived the gulf between conventional Western theology and even the most sophisticated non-European mind:

> Our people fed them with (SPG) High Church orthodoxies and forms which they accepted in a bewildered way, and with (CMS) evangelical orthodoxies which they also accepted, without understanding, for there are very few genuinely 'evangelical' Japanese. The American Protestants fed them with Modernism, resting on criticism and a distant backwash of Harvard Idealism. . . . They did not in the least know what it meant, but it was the latest thing; it looked clever, superior to the orthodoxy of old-fashioned traditionalism. They were hungering for something solid which they could understand. . . .
>
> I laughed at the fine language which attracted them so much . . . made them see its absurdity, and brought them back to the plain issues of faith in the reality of God.[14]

Kelly's own paradoxical wit, wisdom and hard questions commended him to the Japanese as a sage of the Zen Buddhist sort.

China smarted under her defeat by Japan and mounting Western encroachment. To drive out 'foreign devils', secret societies were formed, notably the Righteous Harmony of Fists ('Boxers'), who led the uprising of 1900 in which thousands of foreigners and Chinese Christians perished. Two SPG missionaries were killed; in Peking, Roland Allen, who had been training Chinese for an indigenous ministry, and four others took refuge in the British legation. But by 1912 an independent Chinese Anglican province, the Chung Hua Sheng Kung Hui ('Middle Glorious Holy Common Society') had been formed and—the last Manchu emperor being deposed—a Western-style Republic of China set up, inspired by a Christian, Sun Yat Sen.

Allen came home in 1903 for health reasons. After four years in a parish, he resigned all official Church position and in 1912 published *Missionary Methods: St Paul's or Ours?*,[15] attacking the missionary assumptions of his day as powerfully as Livingstone had done. It was half a century before its time.

In South Africa, the Boers had failed to keep the English out of the Transvaal, and the Church, with SPG help, followed its people. When gold was found on the Witwatersrand in 1886, outsiders poured in: French, Germans, Jews, above all the hated English. These *uitlanders* (who built the great cosmopolitan city of Johannesburg) soon outnumbered the pious Boers four to one and demanded political rights. Africans flocked to the mines for work: many came from Portuguese territory beyond the Lebombo mountains, and in 1893 the diocese of Lembobo[16] was founded for mission to their homeland. In 1899 Boer hostility and *uitlander* ambition exploded in a three-year Boer War. Boer guerrilla tactics evoked from the British a scorched-earth policy and concentration camps. The bitterness of Boer defeat still festers at the roots of Afrikaner nationalism.

To help the Church recover, SPG voted an emergency £6,000 in 1900, £30,000 from its Bicentenary Fund, and £6,000 more after the peace. Before the war, railway missioners had begun ministering to isolated gangers and settlers along the line—a type of mission pioneered by SPG thirty years earlier in India; SPG now provided £1,600 from its Bicentenary Fund and an annual grant for many years thereafter; in 1904 the Province formally adopted the South African Church Railway Mission.[17] In 1904 Archbishop Davidson appealed for funds for Christian education for Europeans, to which SPG contributed £10,000, adding £5,000 for African education. South Africa also received £24,000 from the Pan-Anglican Thank-offering Fund.

In 1910 Britain took a calculated risk, and the uneasy Union of South Africa became a self-governing dominion in the Commonwealth.

During the First World War, SPG managed to maintain all its overseas work. UMCA missionaries in German East Africa were interned, but after their release by Allied troops in 1916, gradually rebuilt the Mission's work. German South-West Africa was mandated to South Africa after the war by the League of Nations. The diocese of Damaraland was set up there in 1924 with SPG support, and the Society began work in Ovamboland in the north.

The impact of the war on non-Europeans was incalculable. Many thousands from all over the British Empire served in its armed forces in Europe. They heard of a war 'to end war' and 'to make the world safe for democracy'; what they saw was a 'Christian' civilisation destroying itself and wantonly slaughtering the flower of its own manhood. In the shock of disillusionment, independence movements in many a colony intensified.

The shock took rather longer to penetrate European consciousness. Unemployed veterans did not exactly experience Britain as a 'land fit for heroes', but high hopes were invested in the League of Nations. The Communist experiment in Russia was hailed by idealists who chose not to see the terrible disciplines of starvation and the concentration camp by which this new utopia was imposed. The collapse of the German mark in 1923 failed to halt an economic vengeance which was preparing the way for a different tyranny. But the sun had not yet set on the British Empire: the White Man's Burden was still being taken up. Committed Christians rejoiced in Church expansion overseas; in the West, unbelievers were the first to perceive that Christendom had been buried in Flanders fields.

Non-Europeans were no longer content with European leadership in Church or State. The Church did more than anyone else to prepare them for independence, especially through its schools. Indigenisation went hand in hand with the change from mission to Church. 'We no longer go out to preach to the heathen in the villages,' wrote Cyril Whitworth, SSM, from Mkuzi in 1926, 'for our whole work is to build up the Church and train the converts that the Church brings to us by her normal life.[18]

That Church must be rooted in the local culture. In India, Bishop Hubback of Assam (1923-48) was ordaining

> men chosen from their villages, the natural leaders of their people, men of devotion, and of love for the people amongst whom they have always lived, whose training[19] consists . . . of a knowledge of the New Testament, and . . . of how to lead the people in reverent worship, a sacra-

mental worship which is independent of literacy or worldly wisdom, and through which even the most backward race can find the Presence of God.[20]

In 1925 UMCA moved St Andrew's College from Zanzibar to Minaki, near Dar es Salaam. Here teacher training could expand and the boys could learn to grow their own food, as they would have to do as village teachers. At Minaki in 1931 Dr Mary Gibbons pioneered a highly successful four-year medical course:

> The country needs doctors, but . . . at the moment the practitioner most useful and easy to fit into the scheme of things is the dispenser-cum-nurse-cum-tribal dresser-cum-agent for sanitation and health . . . a man who can live in a village or district and be able to diagnose simple and common diseases; to perform simple operations, give injections, minister to the health requirements of the village, look after the sanitation, dispense stock mixtures, etc.[21]

Today the need for this sort of 'basic doctor' at the grassroots is increasingly seen in many parts of the world.

How deeply Christian roots had struck was seen in religious communities like the African Society of St John the Baptist (1914) at Tsolo in the Transkei. The wholly indigenous Melanesian Brotherhood, founded in 1925, has sent 125 missionaries to other Pacific countries in the past twenty years and today has a hundred brothers and thirty novices. In India Jack Winslow, Principal of the SPG High School at Ahmednagar 1915-19, felt called to break with the European way of life and attitude of superiority. With SPG help he founded in 1921 the *Christa Seva Sangha* ('Christ Service Society') for worship, study and teaching on the pattern of the Hindu *ashram*, to work among 'untouchables'. In 1927 the CSS moved to Poona, developed student work and a Third Order whose rule was later adopted for the Franciscan Third Order in England.

Nowhere was indigenisation more urgent than in India, where political unrest was growing. The Church often led the way: St Stephen's College, Delhi, was in 1906 the first university college with an Indian principal; the Church of India, Burma and Ceylon achieved independence in 1930, seventeen years before those nations.

Meanwhile Bishop Whitehead of Madras (1899-1922) saw the fulfilment of his dream of an Indian Church under an Indian bishop. In 1903 V.S. Azariah, son of a Tamil priest in Tinnevelly, with two friends started a school among the outcastes in the jungle near Dornakal. So successful were they that in 1909 Azariah was ordained, and in 1912 consecrated Bishop of Dornakal. By 1920 he was in charge of the entire (CMS and SPG) Telugu-speaking mission, which in 1922 became the diocese of Dornakal. Every communicant was asked to take part in an annual week of witness to non-Christian neighbours. At first, inquirers were chiefly outcastes,

> but the change worked in them by conversion was so striking, that their caste neighbours and masters, deeply impressed, began to come for instruction, and were won in numbers unequalled elsewhere.[22]

By 1938 Dornakal had 138 Clergy and 220,000 Christians where thirty-five years before there were none. In 1939 its Cathedral of the Epiphany was consecrated, blending Hindu and Muslim architectural styles under the Cross.

Expanding South African mining and industry drew more and more Africans into the cities as labourers and domestic servants. Miners lived in barrack-like compounds, separated from wife and family for months or years at a time, but at least housed and fed. Priests and catechists worked among them, and many a man returned to his tribe with a Christianity learnt in Kimberley or Johannesburg. Other urban Africans, forbidden to live among Europeans, were segregated in 'locations' or African townships— sprawling shanty-towns without proper roads, drainage or other amenities.

In 1929 Dorothy Maud, a worker in SPG House, felt the call to Africa and with Society help started a settlement in the Johannesburg township of Sophiatown—*Nkutuleni* (House of Peacemaking). She and her helpers lived there, started clubs, classes, a day nursery, a school. Five years later *Leseding* (Place of Light) was opened in Orlando, and the Mirfield Fathers arrived. Through generous gifts, the great churches of St Mary's, Orlando, and Christ the King, Sophiatown, were built. In 1939, with SPG help, Clare Lawrance founded *Tumelong* (Place of Faith) in Lady Selborne, outside Pretoria. In 1944 Miss Maud handed over to the Wantage Sisters four nursery schools, a nursery teacher-training school, seven primary schools, a hospital and innumerable Sunday schools.

> Fighting for the interests of the Natives, missionaries at last moved the municipalities to action, and new townships, better planned and better built, are replacing the worst of the old slums. But the Settlement, with its great church, its schools, its many welfare activities, remains the centre of healthy influences and of promise for the future.[23]

Outside Salisbury, Southern Rhodesia, Barbara Tredgold, who had worked in Johannesburg, in 1947 founded *Runyararo* (House of Peace) in Harari township, along similar lines. With four USPG women missionaries and a large African staff, this remains a vital nerve-centre for the diocese.

In Northern Rhodesia rich reserves of copper were found in 1925 and the same pattern of migrant labour unfolded. Mining towns mushroomed on the Copperbelt: Ndola, Luanshya, Kitwe, Mufulira, Chingola. UMCA began work there in 1930.

To avoid confusion, the major Protestant missionary societies had refrained from entering areas already evangelised by another mission.[24] But this principle of 'comity' (which had never applied in cities anyway) broke down with increasing mobility of populations. The scandal of Christian disunity proved a major obstacle to the Gospel. In 1888 the Lambeth Conference proposed as a basis for Christian unity the 'Lambeth Quadrilateral': the Scriptures as the basis of Christian faith, the Apostles' and Nicene Creeds as sufficient statements of it, the Gospel sacraments of Baptism and the Lord's Supper, and the historic episcopate.

In 1910 a World Missionary Conference met at Edinburgh. Its 1,200 delegates represented missionary societies rather than Churches. (SPG hesitated: would participation compromise its principles? Despite a petition with 900 signatures *against*, at the last moment SPG representation was made official.) There were no Roman Catholics nor Orthodox and only eighteen non-

Europeans, but nothing like it had ever been seen before. In young Azariah of Dornakal the voice of the younger Churches called for Christian unity. The great enthusiasm engendered was expressed in John Mott's slogan 'the evangelisation of the world in this generation'.[25]

National Christian Councils were formed overseas; at home, the Conference of British Missionary Societies (CBMS), which SPG joined in 1918. The International Missionary Council, formed in 1921, held conferences at Jerusalem in 1928 and Tambaram, Madras, in 1938. 'Faith and Order' and 'Life and Work' movements also gathered momentum. The Roman Catholic Church officially held aloof, but the Abbé Paul Couturier launched the movement of prayer for Christian unity, while the Vatican quietly began the massive strengthening of Roman Catholic Biblical scholarship which would make possible its subsequent entry on to the ecumenical scene.

On Montgomery's resignation in 1918, SPG called as Secretary George King, Bishop of Madagascar since 1899. In 1919 the Enabling Act brought the Church Assembly into being with its Missionary Council. Some now said the Church should be its own missionary society, but the societies' view—that the Missionary Council should back their appeals, not initiate a rival one—prevailed. The Council concentrated on education, recruitment, and finding posts at home for returned missionaries.

Next door to SPG House, the Society in 1920 built what is now 64 Great Peter Street, with more library space and a basement for exhibition material. The extra office space, profitably let for forty-five years, would be providentially available for merging SPG and UMCA under one roof.

In 1921 SPG obtained from George V a Second Supplementary Charter. Besides admitting women as Incorporated Members, this put right an extraordinary oversight:

> It has also been represented to Us that the sphere of work of the Society has been extended to parts of the world beyond the seas which do not form part of the Dominions or possessions of the Crown and to people who are not British subjects and also to people of coloured races at

home, and that doubts are felt as to whether such an extension of the operations of the Society was authorized . . . and that it is expedient that such doubts shall be set at rest . . .

It shall be and shall be deemed always to have been lawful for the Society to carry on the work of the Society in all or any parts of the world as the Society may from time to time think proper, and to carry on such work among and for the benefit of persons wheresoever resident and whether British subjects or not and whether at home or abroad, and also to carry on Medical Mission work at home and abroad.

Not only was SPG's work in Madagascar and Mozambique, in China, Japan and Korea retro-actively authorised: the propagation of the Gospel at home and overseas was now by Royal authority declared the single, indivisible task SPG's founders knew it to be. The implications of this, understood and acted upon by Society staff for half a century, are only beginning to be grasped at the grassroots.

The other great landmark of King's Secretaryship was the founding at Selly Oak in 1923 of SPG's College of the Ascension. Since the closing of the Wandsworth hostel in 1913, women missionaries had usually spent a period in study and devotional training at a religious community. Now they would receive a systematic two-year theological training and formation comparable to that given ordinands. The advantages of joining an established group of missionary colleges were obvious, but they were all Free Church: in the aggressively denominational climate of 1923, it is hard to know whose misgivings were greater, SPG's at entering that hot-bed of Nonconformity, or Selly Oak's at the prospect of 'ritualists' in their midst! Time would prove it one of the most important ventures the Society ever made.

In 1925 King was succeeded by the Australian-born Archdeacon of Jerusalem, Percival Stacy Waddy, a man of prayer and energy and a great traveller. The Church Assembly's Missionary Council was then engaged in a 'World Call to the Church' campaign, and in 1926 missionary interest reached its zenith. Contributions to SPG reached £277,643 that year; those to UMCA, £51,530. UMCA began holding summer schools. For six years SPG had to have *two* Royal Albert Hall rallies. The year 1928 saw the start of SPG schools of prayer, and the appointment of Canon W.F. France as Overseas Secretary.

Also in 1928 the Thames flooded the basements of Westminster. SPG's priceless records narrowly escaped destruction. An appeal to the Pilgrim Trust resulted in the opening in 1935 of the Archives Room several flights above the high-water mark and the appointment of a qualified Archivist. The Archives Room is constantly used by inquirers and researchers from all over the world, and the task of indexing the mine of information in the Society's *ten tons* of archives still goes on.

In 1928 Edmund Morgan, then Warden of the College of the Ascension, edited *Essays Catholic and Missionary*,[26] aided by Ernest Spanton, who had come home from Zanzibar in 1925 to succeed Travers as UMCA General Secretary. Many of these essays are now period pieces: there is no shadow of doubt of the superiority of European forms of Christianity and civilisation; the mission station among the 'natives' or 'heathen' is taken for granted; 'Governments' are colonial administrations; Church affairs are London-based. But several are relevant still: Evelyn Underhill's 'Christianity and the Claims of Other Religions', Herbert Kelly's 'Christianity and Education', Morgan's own 'Missionary Vocation and Training'.

From 1919 on, the UMCA story is of expanding opportunity and chronic financial crisis. An era ended with Weston's death in 1924. Four years later the 'Apostle of the Lake', William Johnson (who had joined the Mission in 1876) died at Liuli: at the Africans' request, the name of 'the Venerable William, Confessor' was added to the Nyasaland diocesan calendar and at least one church was dedicated to 'St William Johnson'. At home, recruitment and fund-raising for four dioceses evoked growing activity. The Dartmouth Street office had long been outgrown, and it was decided to invest in bricks and mortar some money put aside against an emergency. A site was bought, and in 1929 Central Africa House was opened at what is now 35 Great Peter Street— right across the road from SPG. UMCA was looking very like a missionary society, though it still saw itself as an African mission with a London outpost.

SPG was building in 1929, too, as the College of the Ascension took permanent form. The necessary £75,000 was all raised by 'Friends', mostly in small donations. ('My mother and I have been saving halfpennies for three months. Now she has added one penny and I have added one, so we have four shillings to give.'[27]) The College, with its uniquely beautiful chapel, went up in a single summer and was opened on 6 October. Three weeks later the Wall Street crash triggered the Great Depression that would end in Hitler's war.

In August 1936, UMCA's Gerald Broomfield came home from Zanzibar, 'sure that his vocation at the moment was to study and write theology'.[28] God and the Mission thought otherwise, for in November Spanton died and Broomfield commenced a quarter-century as UMCA General Secretary. SPG's Stacy Waddy died in 1937 of a fever caught in West Africa. Two brief Secretaryships followed; Noel Hudson (1938-41), former Bishop of Labuan and Sarawak, and John Dauglish (1942-44), former Bishop of Nassau.

A geological shift in theology took place between 1922, when the Doctrine in the Church of England Commission began its work, and 1937, when it published its report. William Temple said in the preface that a theology of Incarnation had given way to a theology of Redemption 'more ready to admit that much in this evil world is irrational and strictly unintelligible' and which 'looks to the coming of the Kingdom as a necessary preliminary to the comprehension of much that now is.'[29] Two years later Temple warned that

> the world of today is one of which no Christian map can be made. It must be changed by Christ into something very unlike itself before a Christian map of it is possible. We used to believe in the sovereignty of God a great deal too light-heartedly.[30]

Before that year was out, Hitler's tanks had rolled into Poland. The rest of the West, safely locating Evil in the charismatic Leader of a nation demonically possessed, went to war with conscience clear. Japanese militarism, too, enabled the dark shadow of industrialism and modern technology to be fought 'out there' by capitalist and communist alike. But an apocalyptic moment of truth was approaching.

The psychic earthquake which has shattered the foundations of Western civilisation first broke the furface in the French Revolution, but because Napoleon met his Waterloo the shock waves did not penetrate the dominant culture until the First World War. At the end of the Second, the culture shock progressed with speed from Belsen and Auschwitz to its blinding climax at Hiroshima on the Feast of the Transfiguration, 1945. A psychic gulf opened between those who saw, and who did not see, the mushroom cloud. It was not only 75,000 Japanese lives that were blasted by The Bomb, but the continuity of history, the credibility of morality, and all the liberal assumptions about rationality and human goodness. After this war, the messengers would have to reconsider not only their methods but their message.

CHAPTER EIGHT

Christian Partnership in a Divided World

*War and after—Partition and unity—The Church
in a broken world—The* Centurion *sails again
Missionary growth in the Angry Fifties
Summoning the People of God—'Towards Freedom'
The Secular Sixties—Changing patterns
of mission—'Mission in SIX Continents'*

IN THE FAR East and South East Asia, some SPG missionaries
got out before the Japanese invasion. Some, with thousands of
other refugees, walked from Burma to India. A few were lost at
sea. Very many were interned. Elsewhere, SPG and UMCA
missionaries battled on despite depleted staffs, commandeered
buildings, shortages, social and economic disruption, spiritual
isolation. It was even possible to start new work: among the
Amerindians of British Guiana SPG in 1942 reopened the remote
Rupununi mission in the south (begun in 1907 but without a
priest for many years) and began new work on the Mazaruni
River near the Venezuelan frontier in the west.

At home, SPG House and Central Africa House had air-raid
shelters within and sandbags without. One bomb scored a direct
hit on a UMCA waste-paper hamper, but failed to explode;
another shattered windows in both buildings; otherwise there
was much anxiety but little damage. Against financial stringency,
home supporters rallied with new efforts, and overseas dioceses
with new economies. Cape Town, Johannesburg and Natal
renounced their SPG grants altogether. The Canadian Church

resolved to forego all further help. The American Church raised £151,352 for the English missionary societies, of which SPG received £39,860 and UMCA £6,650. In 1942 SPG's 86-year-old *Mission Field* was replaced by the more modern and popular *Oversea News*, while UMCA's annual review appeared in more compact form. In 1944 SPG Secretary John Dauglish was succeeded by Basil Roberts, formerly Bishop of Singapore and then Warden of St Augustine's, Canterbury.

After the war, missionaries had to be repatriated and replaced. Vast sums were needed for relief, rebuilding, meeting new challenges. A Far East Relief Fund and a West Indies Appeal were launched. Help, large and small, came from overseas. The Channel Isles had maintained their missionary efforts under German occupation and, when liberated, sent SPG £200. In Canada, a 'consolidation' scheme had begun before the war to build up a £100,000 endowment for the prairie dioceses, part from SPG, part raised locally: the Canadian Church now gave back SPG's £42,000 (plus £6,000 of its own), enabling the Society to start post-war work without delay.

In 1945 Canon France resigned as SPG Overseas Secretary in order to build St Augustine's, Canterbury, into an Anglican Communion staff college. SPG began making training grants for overseas nationals as well as British missionary candidates. In 1946 there came to SPG two men—Edward Sulston as Overseas Secretary and John Dudley Dixon as Home Secretary—whose vision and self-effacing diligence would be behind many developments of the next quarter-century. Gabrielle Hadingham launched the SPG Fellowship, to enlist a deeper level of grassroots support through prayer, study and giving.

One SPG missionary was in Japan throughout the war. Leonora Lea had taught at the Shoin Jo Gakko since 1927. Protected by Bishop Michael Yashiro, she escaped internment. When American bombings burnt three-fourths of Kobe, her house became a refuge. 'What she suffered during those war years and how she survived, we do not know; she never talked about it . . . We only know that Bishop Yashiro's wife, like many others, died of starvation.'[1]

After the war the Nippon Sei Ko Kai asked foreign help only with rebuilding shattered churches and, for a time, stipends of bishops and theological college staff; SPG gave £15,000. Leonora Lea reorganised the Shoin Jo Gakko, adding a college department, then became head of St Michael's International School in Kobe, founded by Yashiro as an act of reparation for the war. In 1968 she was decorated by the Emperor for her educational work.

But there was a spiritual vacuum in post-war Japan. Seven hundred new religions sprang up in the sixties (the 'rush hour of the gods') as people groped for meaning in a consumer society. Just before her death in 1971, Leonora Lea wrote how the Japanese imitate the West, but 'can't grasp that some of us really take God seriously: They think we "take up" religion as a branch of culture, like taking up art, music, fencing, photography or pottery.' Of course many in the West do just that.

And some Japanese take God seriously. Michael Yashiro, trained by the SSM as Kelham, was one of the missionary giants of our time, a mighty reconciler of men to one another and to God. Leonora Lea visited him in hospital in October 1970, a week before that gallant Samurai warrior for Christ died of cancer. Barely able to speak, he took pencil and paper.

> He drew a circle in the top left corner and wrote 'Personal Soul'—then half of Dr Batchelor's name (a former missionary in Hokkaido) and said, 'He and my father and I made 2,000 Christians—each soul.' Then he drew a line down the left side of the paper, and across the bottom made a series of rectangles . . . As each was completed he gave it a name: 'Committees—slogans—resolutions—policies—you understand? All are secular, secular—ordinary business world—no good in Church—lead back to the secular world.' And he drew a line up the right side to the top right corner and said again, 'Secular.' Then he drew lines from the 'Secular World' across the top of the page to the 'personal soul' and said: 'Only way is to speak straight to each soul—speak to each . . . You understand? Tell archbishops, tell all, all, all, to speak to souls—one soul—bring to Christ—my last message.' He dropped the pen and lay exhausted. Tears poured down his face. *'Tell—everybody.'*

In 1944 UMCA lost one of its last links with its beginnings: John Swedi. Just before his death, Swedi attended Bishop Baker's enthronement in Zanzibar Cathedral. 'I remember being sold as a slave, just here,' said this last of the five boys given to the Mission by the Sultan in 1864.[2]

In Northern Rhodesia, 1947 saw the founding of St John's Seminary in Lusaka and St Francis' Hospital at Katete. In Tanganyika a new hospital was built in 1951 at Mkomaindo (the original 'Masasi'); in 1952, a teacher-training college for women at Magila. In 1953 the ill-fated Central Africa Federation began, and the Province of Central Africa united Nyasaland and Northern Rhodesia with the SPG-linked dioceses of Mashonaland and Matabeleland. On Lake Nyasa, financial stringency compelled in 1956 the sale of that faithful carrier of fishers of men, the *Chauncy Maples*; it became, appropriately, the mother ship of a fishing fleet.[3] On the home front, the Friends of UMCA were started for prayer, study, and support of the Mission.

In 1947, non-European nations began taking their places in the British Commonwealth. India was to be the first, but the unity imposed on the Indian subcontinent by the British Empire proved as deceptive as the Roman unification of Europe from Scotland to Sicily. Hindu-Muslim hostility is as old as the Moghul Empire. As Moghul power declined, the British Raj took over; with independence, the age-old enmity surfaced; 300 million Hindus feared domination again by a militant minority; 90 million Muslims feared absorption into Hinduism. Partition resulted, with a massive exchange of populations and communal riots in which three million perished.

In Delhi St Stephen's Hospital found itself at the crossroads of chaos as Hindus and Muslims fled in opposite directions. Seventy thousand Muslim refugees camped outside would trust no one but Christians; later, destitute Hindus arrived from Pakistan. The witness of its equal care for all had much to do with the atmosphere of religious tolerance afterwards in Pakistan.

Burma, which achieved independence in 1947, opted out of the Commonwealth; SPG's work there continued. In Ceylon (independent in 1948) the Society's work had ended in 1929.

The Church of India, Pakistan, Burma and Ceylon (CIPBC) maintained its supra-national unity despite political divisions. SPG's 1947 India Consolidation Scheme, adopted by most North Indian dioceses, helped strengthen local autonomy and self-support: for ten years capital grants for investment gradually replaced annual grants; since the investments produced only about half the income surrendered, local giving was stimulated.

The Church of South India (CSI) was inaugurated in 1947 after twenty-eight years of negotiations. Its architect was Azariah of Dornakal:

> We must have *one* Church, a Church of India which can be our spiritual home, where the Indian religious genius can find natural expression, a living branch of the Holy, Catholic, Apostolic Church, the visible symbol of unity in a divided land, drawing all men to our Blessed Lord. . . . Unity may be theoretically desirable in Europe and America; it is vital to the Church in the mission field.[4]

Four Anglican dioceses, three of them SPG-aided, united with the British Methodists and the South India United Church, formed in 1910 by Congregationalists and Presbyterians. The CSI way of uniting existing episcopal and non-episcopal ministries caused great dissension. Many SPG supporters felt they could not support the CSI which was not then in communion with the Church of England; many others wished to do so. The Society has no views on faith and order other than those of the Church it serves, but on this that Church was deeply divided. What was to be done?

SPG decided that, apart from aid to inter-denominational institutions, it could only support individual missionaries in the CSI, with funds earmarked by donors for a CSI Separate Account.[5] The Nandyal Archdeaconry of Dornakal refused to enter CSI: these 'continuing Anglicans' were looked after by the CIPBC, of which in 1963 Nandyal became a diocese, and with which in 1970 it entered the Church of North India.

Relations with the Church of England slowly improved. In 1959 CSI Bishop Lesslie Newbigin wrote that 'the pastoral ministry of bishops has come to be the great unifying factor. They have come to be accepted as fathers in God.'[6] SPG's CSI

Separate Account was replaced by the CSI Aid Fund, still for earmarked donations only. At last in 1973, at the request of the Archbishop of Canterbury, financial help to CSI (now in full communion with the Church of England) was made a charge on USPG's General Fund.

The traditional Protestant view of mission as primarily evangelisation of individuals dominated ecumenical thinking until just before the Second World War, when the Catholic view of mission as planting the Church where it does not yet exist took over. (SPG's aim had in good Anglican fashion embraced both from the start.) Rediscovery of the corporate dimension of Christian experience both evoked and was evoked by the Liturgical Movement, which enjoyed its greatest relevance at this time. In 1948 the 'Faith and Order' and 'Life and Work' movements merged into the World Council of Churches (WCC). The *Church* was the focus of ecumenical thought and action—almost to the exclusion of the world.

That world in 1948 was falling apart. Britain formally withdrew from Palestine an authority already abdicated in fact; the State of Israel was proclaimed, as sporadic terror erupted into war. There was barbed wire where they crucified our Lord. It was in Jerusalem that the impotence of the United Nations was revealed when its representative, Count Bernadotte, was murdered in broad daylight—and nothing happened. The 'Cold War' began; Germany and Korea were partitioned; Communist coups took over Czechoslovakia and Hungary; the twelve-year 'Emergency' (guerrilla war) in Malaya was at its height. In South Africa a Nationalist Government began to enact its *apartheid* policy into law.

In 1949 Mao Tse-Tung's Communists won control of China, ending a half-century of anarchy: Chaing Kai Shek's Nationalists, having failed to deal with feudal warlords, famine and inflation, banditry in the countryside and corruption in government, lost the 'mandate of heaven'; China looked for a government that could *govern*—and restore her self-sufficiency and self-respect.

Churches were at first unmolested, but by 1951 violent anti-foreign reaction compelled all expatriates to leave. The 'Three-

Self' reforms then imposed (self-government, self-support, self-propagation) are only what all missionaries should work for: such a policy had been urged by Roland Allen in 1912. But the cutting off of fellowship (apart from prayer) between Christians in China and elsewhere impoverishes us all, for there is much to be learnt from the Chinese experiment, despite its ambivalence.

The human cost of freedom from anarchy and from mass-starvation and illiteracy has been compulsory mediocrity and the crushing of dissent: who can say how it compares with the human cost of Western commercial and industrial 'development'? A regimented life leaves little leisure or privacy (though freedom of religion is theoretically guaranteed) and the Gospel according to Mao is religiously propagated, but freedom and individuality were little valued in Confucian China. The great Maoist error may well prove to be not so much the answers given to the needs of the moment as the questions refused by trying to stop the clock of history in the middle of the Exodus. Meantime,

> we have to abandon the fantasy, if we still cherish it, that when we meet the Christians in China we shall find them disillusioned with communism and secretly opposed to the regime. . . . If we cannot countenance the possibility of a Christian thanking God for the Maoist ideals and way of life, in spite of the ambiguities in it, we had better keep away from China.[7]

China's was the first door to be slammed in the face of Western missionaries. The shock waves would penetrate deep into missionary theology.

The Korean Church had grown greatly in the 1930s under Bishop Cecil Cooper's leadership. In 1945 Cooper and several other missionaries returned to help with reconstruction. American troops occupied the south; Russians the north. The Church was destitute and inflation rampant. Currency restrictions forbade transfer of sterling, but in 1948 an unaccountably sport-minded SPG voted a £5,000 subsidy for Korean athletes at the Olympic Games in London, and some uncommonly mission-minded sport enthusiasts in Korea collected £5,000 for Bishop Cooper. . . .

Once the bishop was able to visit the three priests in the Russian zone, who (though doing secular work) were continuing

107

their ministry. In Seoul the theological college reopened and a student centre and hostel were planned. But in 1950 war came again, and a flood of refugees from the north. Cooper survived three years' imprisonment; five priests and a nun perished. The crucifix on the cathedral door was used for target practice. One of the Church's greatest tasks after this war was the care of war orphans. Korea's thousands of beggar children remain a major concern today.

SPG's year-long, world-wide 250th birthday party was a tremendous stimulus to the Church. Eipscopal envoys to America, Canada, the Caribbean, Australia and New Zealand, Africa, India, and East Asia conveyed SPG's thanksgiving for the past and resolution for the future, while a team of overseas nationals reminded the Church in Britain just how widespread was the Anglican Communion SPG had helped to found.

Pat Stacy Waddy's popular history of SPG, *A Ship Under Sail*, had been published in 1950.[8] In 1951 H.P. Thompson's full-scale *Into All Lands* was greeted by the *Times Literary Supplement* as the record of 'a great religious and social movement for the benefit of humanity, sustained mainly by private enterprise in the face of vast official apathy.' The *Church Times* called it 'a most handsome autobiography . . . a magnificent justification of the Society's ancient title, the handmaid of the Church, the nursing mother of churches.'

Greetings poured in from overseas. The most poignant, from the now isolated Chinese Church, noted how SPG had

> witnessed to God's work throughout the world and con-
> trived a movement of liberation. . . . West to the New
> World, East to Asia, South to Australia, North to the
> Eskimos, the SPG exalted the Messiah and refused not even
> martyrdom.[9]

The CBMS admired

> the way you so readily confer administrative responsibility
> on the bishops and diocesan authorities on the field: the
> way you make large consolidation grants . . . to enable
> them to launch out independently of your direction, the
> generous and personal way in which you care for your

missionary colleagues, and your continuing interest in the spiritual welfare of British people overseas. The concern of SPG for the encouragement of indigenous Christian art is well-known, and the publications in this field have greatly stimulated general interest.[10] The worth and dignity of worship, the practice of personal devotion, the emphasis on the centrality of our Lord and His Church, the gracious ministry of women, the skill and compassion of Christian doctors and nurses, all shine for us in your service overseas.[11]

But what caught the imagination of a war-weary, rationed country was the most exuberant visual aid in the Society's history: a half-scale working model of HMS *Centurion*, which had carried Keith to America in 1702. In the summers of 1951 and 1952, this 'Gospel ship' (flying the flags of thirty-eight countries where SPG was working) made missionary voyages around the coast of Britain. She was the focus of open-air preaching, civic receptions, processions of witness, packed services, exhibitions, films, bookstalls, personal evangelism. The *Centurion* appeared in newspapers and on the new television: 'One of the most powerful ventures of evangelism in recent times', said SPG Editorial Secretary Kenneth Symcox. 'The Church was doing something, and doing it with vigour and imagination.'[12] An estimated 250,000 Britons heard the Gospel preached from *Centurion*'s deck by men of many nations. 'We may no longer think of missionary work in terms of distant places of the earth.'[13]

The year of celebration began on 16 June 1951 with a Eucharist in St Paul's Cathedral, a vast garden party at Lambeth Palace, and the blessing of the *Centurion* at Lambeth Pier. At an Albert Hall rally two days later Archbishop Fisher referred to mission as 'both the expression of a living faith and a prime creator of it.'[14] On 19 July four new stained-glass windows were dedicated in the SPG Chapel, replacing war-shattered ones and commemorating the first Anglican bishops of African, Indian, Chinese and Japanese race. A thank-offering of £10,317 from overseas was presented at a great closing service in St Paul's on 14 June 1952.

One of the birthday envoys represented SPG at the inauguration of the Province of West Africa, which united the CMS mission fields of Nigeria and Sierra Leone with the SPG-assisted dioceses of Accra and 'Gambia and the Rio Pongas'. On SPG's 250th birthday, the West Indian mission, begun as a thank-offering for its 150th anniversary and its own 1752 venture on 'the coast of Guiney' had come of age.

In 1952 the first H-bomb exploded. The following year, the Coronation managed (just) to recapture the mood of Christendom; we shall not see its like again. In 1954 Vietnam was divided. 1956 saw the Hungarian uprising crushed, and the Suez crisis. In Britain teddy boys, rock 'n' roll and 'angry young' writers emerged from the now-articulate 'lower orders' to disturb and shock. The Campaign for Nuclear Disarmament began.

The Angry Fifties were a decade of growth for SPG. Though income never remotely matched needs, it rose dramatically in 1951 to £455,473. But the pound had been devalued in 1949. In some places overseas, costs were up 500 per cent. 'Twentieth century missions cost twentieth century money,' observed Editorial Secretary Dewi Morgan.[15] Between 1947 and 1957 SPG sent over a million pounds to India alone. A Third Supplementary Charter in 1956 gave more flexibility in investment and more freedom in transferring overseas property to overseas Churches.

By the mid-fifties, 5,000 SPG Fellowship members were defining their aims as 'Study, Pray, Give'. The Society was producing much study material for both adults and children, including filmstrips and films. For those for whom 'Give' might also mean 'Go', there was the Association of Missionary Candidates (AMC), started in 1952 by Men Candidates' Secretary Paul Ashwin;[16] in the still-separate Women Missionaries and Candidates' Department, a parallel women's AMC was begun by Elizabeth Ferrar.

Lloyd George once referred to the West Indies as 'the slums of the British Empire'. Most Caribbean problems are rooted in a history of which nobody is proud. Except for mainland Amerindians, all Caribbean peoples have come from somewhere else. Legacies of slavery include foreign economic domination, local apathy, unstable family life, one-crop economies, and a deep identity-crisis. An enervating climate, vulnerability to hurricanes,

110

and vast distances also pose problems.[17] And the thing about islands is that they are insular.

After the war many West Indians sought work abroad. In 1952, United Stated immigration restrictions diverted these 'brown British' to what they thought was their mother country. They knew that planters had never taken Christianity seriously, but surely in Britain people practised what they preached? The depth of their disillusionment is indicated by the fact that, though sixty-seven per cent of West Indians now in Britain attended 'mainstream' Churches at home, only five per cent do so in Britain.

In 1954-5 Bishop and Mrs Roberts toured the Caribbean together. (In those days SPG was married to the Mothers' Union, of which Mrs Roberts was President. Much of the MU's excellent overseas work has in fact been done in collaboration with SPG, UMCA and USPG.) Their tour led to SPG's West Indies Appeal, which raised £57,469, mostly for schools. In 1956 the Mirfield Fathers took over the running of Codrington Theological College, at last fulfilling Codrington's dream.[18]

In South Africa, rapid industrialisation created problems for the Church. Martin Knight, SSM, wrote in 1952 that the new mining town of Welkom—a village of 700 five years before—had 14,000 whites and 20,000 blacks and would soon have 310,000, all of them uprooted. For the African, 'in the Reserve the Church was there to sanctify his home life. Here the Church must *be* his home.'[19] But all problems are multiplied by *apartheid*. Effective protest is prevented by the Suppression of Communism Act, which by failing to define 'communism' allows the Government to silence *anyone*. In 1954 the Bantu Education Act limited the education allowed to Africans: 'There is no place for the Bantu in European society above the level of certain forms of labour.'[20] And since the white standard of living would collapse without cheap black labour, there is no true 'separate development'.

Rather than comply, the Church gave up its African schools. Many schools were used also for worship and social activity. SPG, which in 130 years had already sent nearly £3½ million to South Africa, now found, in addition to its 1954 annual grant of £65,000, a further £25,000 for Church family centres, diocesan

111

directors of religious education, and ordination training. It also raised a South African Emergency Fund of £40,000 for simple vernacular literature and to finance St Augustine's Test School for African ordinands. Established at Modderpoort under the care of the SSM, this gave preliminary training in language, clear thinking, and devotional discipline.

Racial tension was also building up in the Central Africa Federation. In 1957 Gonville ffrench-Beytagh, then Dean of Salisbury, wrote that

> neither of the two peoples we desire to bring into partnership really desire it very much. Each of them keeps on talking about his rights. When two lots of people talk about their rights, then you have trouble. The fact of the matter, of course, is that no human being has any rights at all. He has only duties. And it is very hard for a politician to say so.[21] If partnership between Black and White is to happen in Central Africa or anywhere else, it is dependent, first of all, upon the conversion of the people. And that is the Church's duty.[22]

Early in 1957 Bishop Roberts died. His successor, Bishop Eric Trapp of Zululand, saw the need for a new approach if the Society was to help the Church break out of the straitjacket of the post-war years. In 1958 SPG raised an extra £36,000 for some urgent new overseas projects, while its study and prayer material focused attention on the Lambeth conference, which proclaimed: 'Every generation needs to be evangelised, and to this all-important task we summon the People of God in every land'. SPG House (always a 'left luggage' office for Lambeth Conferences) arranged regional discussion groups of bishops, who laid bare as never before the true immensity and urgency of their needs. In 1959 a joint letter to all English incumbents from the eleven recognised missionary societies asked

> what answer is to be given to the evident call of the Holy Spirit to our Church at this time, to send its messengers into all the world with the Gospel message, on a scale and with a degree of sacrificial backing never before envisaged or attempted?

'Nothing less than a great new surge forward will be adequate,' said a subsequent joint letter from SPG and CMS. Spurred by the societies, the Church Assembly in 1960 called for an unprecedented increase in prayer, manpower and money for the Church overseas.[23]

'Summoning the People of God' was the theme of SPG's own surge forward in the next five years. In 1959 it reorganised its finances into an ongoing 'Budget of Commitment' and a supplementary 'Budget of Opportunity' for launching new work. In 1960 the Projects scheme invited parishes, in addition to their regular giving, to raise a fixed amount annually for a *particular* person or need, receiving in return regular, detailed news: by 1973 this scheme, which still continues, had raised nearly a million pounds and greatly stimulated interest and prayer. Beginning in 1962, *Prayer Is My Job* (an imaginative series of sets of illustrated prayer leaflets) for ten years helped many thousands to organise a regular offering of prayer time.

In 1962 South Africa speeded up implementation of the Group Areas Act. Entire townships were forcibly transplanted to new areas where sites available for churches would be forfeited if not used quickly. If the South African Church (which itself raised £100,000) was to follow its people, a hundred new churches must be built *at once*. SPG voted £230,000 in grants and loans—the biggest allocation of funds in its history—to help start sixty-five new parishes. Its Promotion & Training Secretary, Frank Cooper, toured South Africa, helping Churchmen of all races to organise their own missionary obedience.

All over the world, evangelistic opportunities that might never come again called for action on a scale quite beyond local reserves. To 'hasten' the pace of overseas development, SPG launched in 1963 a revolving loan fund called FESTINA. Individuals having money not needed at the moment, but which they could not afford to give, were invited to lend it through the Society, interest free; in eight years £300,000 was raised and a hundred loans made. This 'Anglican family bank' continues to grow.

All these efforts bore much fruit. Between 1959 and 1964 the Society's income nearly doubled, making possible (over and above ongoing commitments) some one million pounds' worth of exciting and significant new developments. 1961 saw twice as many offers of service as for many years past: in 1963, 135 new missionaries were sent overseas. SPG's experience in these years of growth was to be shared with the world-wide Church in the Toronto Anglican Congress of 1963.

UMCA kept its centenary in 1957-8. At an Albert Hall rally on 4 June 1957, Canon Broomfield set forth the centenary theme:

> Physical slavery was . . . no more than a symptom of an all-embracing servitude which held Africa in bondage. Poverty and disease, ignorance and superstition, false ideas of the world, of the nature of man and of God, fettered and enthralled both mind and spirit. Livingstone urged that Africa should be led TOWARDS FREEDOM—towards the freedom which only Christ can give.[24]

John Kingsnorth, home from Northern Rhodesia, stressed the urgency, in the rising tide of black and white nationalisms, of seizing the immense opportunities of the moment. In Westminster Abbey in May 1958, Bishop Nigel Cornwall of Borneo, formerly a priest in Masasi, reminded those gathered near Livingstone's grave that 'the time had come when the Mission must give way to the Church, rooted in the soil and with African husbandmen'.[25] The three-volume *History of the UMCA*, published in 1957 (incorporating the 1909 volume with two new ones by Canon Blood), closes with some words spoken by Charles Gore, as President of the Mission, at the blessing of Central Africa House in 1929:

> We have always maintained that what we were about was not the transporting of Anglicanism into Africa, but the building up of an African Catholic Church. And the Africans caught the fire of that idea.[26]

The 'wind of change' of Macmillan's 1960 speech blew mainly from Ghana, in 1957 the first British colony in Africa to win independence. Africanisation of the Church in UMCA areas proceeded in an atmosphere of political revolution. In 1959 UMCA's Mozambique work joined with SPG's in the diocese of Lebombo. Next year the province of East Africa united UMCA's Tanganyika dioceses with CMS-supported ones in Tanganyika and Kenya. Tanganyika's political independence followed in 1961. In

114

1964 the Zanzibar Africans revolted against their Arab rulers and joined the now-renamed Tanzania. In Mozambique the 'Frelimo' guerrilla war for independence from Portugal began. The Central African Federation broke up as Nyasaland became independent Malawi, and Norther Rhodesia, independent Zambia.

Britain refused to grant (Southern) Rhodesia independence without majority rule. In 1965 the white minority, outnumbered by Africans twenty to one, made their own unilateral declaration of independence. Declining to use force, Britain imposed economic sanctions. The Rhodesia regime, supported by South Africa, began to entrench itself, notably by the Land Tenure Act of 1969, which apportioned the land 'equally'—half to a quarter-million Europeans, half to five and a quarter million Africans.[27]

The last of the great UMCA cathedrals—Holy Cross, Lusaka—was completed in time for Zambia's independence celebrations. In the post-Christendom dispersion of today's West, some doubt the value of cathedrals and 'great churches'. But Africa is still building Christendom. An SPG missionary watching the African crowd at the consecration of Johannesburg Cathedral in 1929 summed it up:

> Here was a soul finding at long last a body in which for the first time it could really expand and function. . . . The congregations of a hundred poor little wood and iron churches gathered for the moment into one great whole.[28]

The Church-centred era reached its climax at New Delhi in 1961 when the World Council of Churches merged with the International Missionary Council. Ecumenism, reinforced by Biblical scholarship across denominational lines, received a huge new stimulus from the Second Vatican Council (1962-5). The Church now filled its own horizon almost to the exclusion of the world.

Yet ever since the 'China shock' theologians had been wrestling with the relationship between God's work in his Church and his work in secular history. (It was bad form to suggest that the Devil might also be at work.) God's mission was distinguished from our missions, now seen as historically conditioned responses. It was no longer just 'Christ and his Church' but a fully

Trinitarian theology: God sends his Son and his Spirit, and his apostles through the Son and by the Spirit. The emphasis shifted from mission as a function of God's Church to the Church as a function of God's mission.

Now, you cannot 'crusade for Christ' when Jesus is already revered by millions outside the Church, or 'plant the Church among the heathen' when the Church is often present in forms which contradict the Gospel message. What should the messengers do now?

There was more to the wind of change than politics. Western civilisation had lost its intellectual and moral frame of reference, though its technology went marching on. It was not only religious language which the builders of towers to heaven and utopias on earth brainwashed us into finding meaningless, but *all* language. Prostituted to the lies of advertising and propaganda, rational speech and thought themselves disintegrated. We were bombarded with images and deprived of the silence and solitude in which to assimilate them. We no longer had a vernacular into which to translate Bible or liturgy, only clichés and jargon (those modern forms of Gnosticism), remote from flesh and blood. How can those who regress to the pre-verbal perception of infancy hear the Word, or speak of God?

In 1963 the theological ferment exploded into popular view with *Honest to God*. The faithful cried, 'They have taken away my Lord, and I know not where they have laid him.' A 'secular Gospel' was preached, and 'religionless Christianity' practised, by those who found their priestly role suspended between an inconceivable God and a crumbling community. The Church experienced a collective dark night of the soul.

After the 'death of God', what? In the Holy Saturday vigil we watch by the grave of God while Christ plumbs the depths and by his presence there destroys the alienation from God which is hell. There is darkness on the face of the deep, but there will come the New Fire and the passage through the waters to new life: 'Fear not (says Moses to the terrified rabble by the Red Sea); *stand still*, and see the salvation of God.' Nothing was more distasteful to secular man in the sixties. Yet behind its technological bravado the over-confident West began at last to perceive its own dark shadow.

116

Indigenisation of overseas Churches accelerated, with growing emphasis on theological and lay training. In 1956 John Daly, for fifteen years Bishop of Gambia and for six of Accra, was called to Korea. At once he called for a 'Three-Self' movement and began building up the Korean ministry. In 1958 SPG helped rebuild St Michael's Theological College in Seoul. The little Korean Sisterhood of the Holy Cross flourished and grew. When the diocese was divided in 1965, Paul Lee, the first Korean bishop, was consecrated for the senior see of Seoul. Daly's successor as Bishop of Taejon, Richard Rutt, would be the last English bishop in Korea.

In Burma in 1956 SPG helped reopen Holy Cross Theological College in Rangoon. Two years later it brought to the College of the Ascension for a year Esther Hla Gyaw, who went home to build up a flourishing Anglican Young People's Association which is one of the growing-points of the Burmese Church. In 1964 (two years after the revolutionary government took over) the diocese proclaimed a 'Three-Self' policy and was ready when in 1966 all foreigners had to leave. Withdrawal of expatriates greatly stimulated Burmese leadership. USPG still shares financially in the work of this vigorous Church—how vigorous, can be seen from its list of *lay* responsibilities: [29]

> conducting prayers in church and at home, preaching, witnessing, and intelligent sharing in the sacraments; understanding evangelism and responsible sharing in it; understanding stewardship, practising economy at home, economic uplifting of parishioners and of the Church, getting the habit of saving for the Church; knowing the Bible and prayer book, being up on current affairs, knowing what the Church's initiatives are; honesty, self-criticism, forgiveness, freedom from hatred, fostering goodwill and neighbourliness, avoiding greed and discrimination; reading spiritual literature, praying and caring for the spiritual welfare of others.

In Africa, mission stations were turning into parishes with local clergy. Church schools and hospitals were, as earlier in England, increasingly taken over by governments, leaving Churches free to pioneer new ways of service. In some very poor countries, however, outside help will be needed for a long time:

as recently as 1974 Malawi warned that it *could* not in the for-seeable future take over the half of its hospitals now run by Churches,[30] and in Central America Belize said the same of Church schools there.

Nowhere is the ambivalence of all human achievement more starkly seen than in Christian medical work, which by lowering infant mortality and lengthening life expectancy has inescapably contributed to today's population explosions. Family planning and community development have become integral parts of most overseas medical work, along with preventive medicine and fighting malnutrition. Dr Kathleen Wright, USPG's Medical Secretary, noted in 1974 that 'the trend now is very much away from curative institutions, which only serve a minority of the population, towards taking positive health to the people through community health schemes.'[31]

In India in the 1950s an industrial revolution exploded south-west of the Ganges. The area centres on Calcutta, India's commercial capital and greatest seaport (with the world's largest university and the world's worst slums), but most of this 'Ruhr of India' is in the tribal diocese of Chota Nagpur. Great steel cities mushroomed where tigers used to prowl. Ranchi grew from 40,000 to 400,000. Durgapur, once a sleepy village, in nine years drew 1½ million workers from all over India, speaking a Babel of languages. Villagers who had never worn shoes learnt the mechanical rhythms of factories; their wives, the loneliness of vast housing estates. In the mid-1960s USPG was involved in setting up the Ecumenical Social and Industrial Institute in Durgapur, and in similar work in Nagpur, Kanpur and, later, on the Jurong Industrial Estate in Singapore.

> If Anglicans really believe that the Catholic Church is best organised as a fellowship of autonomous churches, they must embody that conviction in their own common life, so that younger and poorer churches will be helped to achieve full and responsible autonomy and the resources developed within each will be made available for the enrichment of all.[32]

This conclusion of the whole Anglican Communion at Toronto

in 1963 SPG had half-consciously practised since 1701 and systematically tested since Lambeth 1958. The Toronto document embodying it unfortunately emerged from drafting several pages longer than most people's span of attention, under the jaw-breaking title 'Mutual Responsibility and Inter-dependence in the Body of Christ', and linked with a call for a specific sum (£5 million) of new money for mission. Predictably, 'MRI' was widely misinterpreted as bigger and better fund-raising on the old pattern.

The Archbishop of Canterbury had got it right in his opening sermon:

> We must plan our mission together, and use our resources in the service of our single task. The word 'missionary' will mean not colonialism of any kind, but going to one another to help one another. Let African and Asian missionaries come to England to help convert the post-Christian heathenism in our country and to convert our English Church to a closer following of Christ. [33]

The WCC Division of World Mission and Evangelism, meeting that summer in Mexico City, coined the phrase 'Mission in *Six* Continents': it was no longer to be 'sending' and 'receiving' Churches, but God's one mission in one world. A dozen years later, the implications of this are only just beginning to be worked out.

All sorts of mutually beneficial direct relationships between dioceses across the world resulted from Toronto, going far beyond financial considerations to fellowship in prayer, consultation and sharing of personnel. But the Congress missed Archbishop Ramsey's main point, though he repeated his text like a refrain: 'O God, thou art my God; early will I seek thee.' Proclaiming adoration of God to be our 'first privilege and final goal', he went straight to the root both of the modern world's agony, in its alienation from God, and of our missionary inadequacy:

> 'As the soul is in the body, so are the Christians in the world.' By lifting up their souls in the simplicity of love towards God, Christians are doing on the world's behalf what the world has lost the power to do, and they are serving the world by helping it to recover the soul which it

has lost. To say this is no platitude. Rather is it a priority which the Church is all too ready to neglect. In the noise of our time there is little enough of the quite waiting upon God which is the heart of our religion. In the activities of our Church life there is a forgetfulness that the reality of God is not necessarily made known by the multiplying of the things we do. We need to be recalled to St Dominic's great description of the Christian way: *contemplare et contemplata aliis tradere*, to contemplate and to pass on to others the things contemplated. Is our weakness in the second due to our being often too busy for the first?[34]

Nobody seemed to hear. A dozen years later, the world's thirst for the Living God is too apparent for even ecclesiastics to ignore much longer.

CHAPTER NINE

One Mission in One World

---

*The United Society–Partnership in training
and education–Restructuring and reassessment
Theology, politics and economics*

BROOMFIELD'S RETIREMENT as UMCA General Secretary in 1961 marked the end of the era when bishops in Africa looked to London for guidance: all UMCA work was in autonomous Churches. What now was the Mission's role? Was the day of its exclusive link with a particular area over?

All this was under discussion when Canon John Kingsnorth succeeded Broomfield. His office looked straight across Great Peter Street into Bishop Trapp's.

> Often one of the two, seeing his opposite number free of visitors, would pick up the phone and discuss a common problem or a common joy. And again and again the question nagged, as it did with other members of the staff and with supporters all over the country . . . why should the societies remain apart?[1]

In July 1963, both societies resolved to discuss a possible merger with each other and 'with any other Anglican missionary society that desired it'. Trapp's vision, shared by both senior staffs, was that merging UMCA and SPG might draw all the Anglican societies together.

On 1 January 1965, after eighteen months of prayer, planning and litigation, SPG and UMCA died and were reborn as the *United* Society for the Propagation of the Gospel, with Trapp as

Secretary and Kingsnorth as Deputy Secretary; ('We're all Trappists now,' quipped one ex-UMCA-er.) All geographical reference was dropped: the United Society existed (as SPG's 1921 Charter affirmed) to propagate the Gospel *anywhere*. [2]

> We are servants of the Church—overseas and at home. We have no vested interest in the preservation of our own charters or our own identity. We have certain skills and a certain fund of experience which we want to be at the service of the whole Church. If the Church desires USPG to continue as she is and to flourish—good: if the Church desires that USPG shall die, and a wider unified society be born—good: if the Church desires that USPG and all other societies shall give way to new forms of mission structure— it is equally good. [3]

An inaugural Eucharist was celebrated in Westminster Abbey, near Livingstone's grave.

In the following months, frequent but goodnaturedly corrected slips of the tongue testified to a deep sense of continuity. The SPG Fellowship and Friends of UMCA were now Friends of USPG, re-defining their aims as Understand, Share, Pray, Go. *Oversea News* and *Central Africa* had given way to *Network*; King's Messengers and Coral League, to Adventurers. On 8 May, 7,000 supporters converged on the Alexandra Palace for an exuberant but administratively somewhat traumatic festival (the 'Ally Pally Rally') at which the Archbishop of Canterbury presided, Bishop Trapp celebrated and the Dean of Westminster preached from a platform held up (just) by a quantity of beer-crates, and such a joyful noise was made unto the Lord that BBC-TV News looked in from next door to see what was up.

The United Society's third constituent body, the Cambridge Mission to Delhi, joined in 1968.

The College of the Ascension closed in 1964 to reconsider its role. No missionary achievement was more revolutionary than the demonstration by countless women missionaries of a dignified, useful place in society for the single woman. But as more local nurses and teachers were trained overseas, fewer women missionaries were wanted, and, with earlier marriage, fewer volunteered. Indigenous bishops actually asked for *more* expatriate help (a measure of Western failure to train enough local leadership), but—save for the perennial shortage of doctors—of different kinds. Experienced trainers-of-others were wanted, and specialists to pioneer industrial mission, university chaplaincies, youth work, agricultural training, community development. It was the heyday of the short-term expert, who could hardly be expected to spend two years in missionary training. And in the theological climate of the sixties, those keenest to serve human need overseas under Christian auspices did not necessarily see evangelism as part of their calling.

The College reopened in 1965 to train men and women for mission *anywhere*[4] through a variety of courses available in Selly Oak, studies being arranged to meet individual need. Few now spent more than a year there, many only a term or two. Increasing difficulties over visas and work permits made clear that the number of Britons serving overseas was going to diminish, but growing numbers of overseas nationals now came to train for mission in their own countries: the proportion of USPG training grants for such students rose dramatically, as did grants to build up theological and lay training overseas. St Augustine's, Canterbury, closed as the Anglican Communion staff college in 1967; in 1969 the College of the Ascension invited applications from anywhere, not just from USPG-linked overseas dioceses.

In 1968 the Selly Oak missionary colleges together set up the Centre for Training in Christian Mission, closely linked with nearby Birmingham University. Selly Oak's 800-odd student body now represents several dozen countries. Lectures, seminars, and practical experience of mission in Darkest Birmingham are fully ecumenical.

Co-operation among the Anglican missionary societies had grown in the 1950s and '60s, especially in education. Since 1963 their General Secretaries and Home Secretaries have met regularly as groups, as well as in the CBMS and the Missionary and Ecumenical Council of Church Assembly (MECCA) and its successor, the General Synod's Board of Mission and Unity (BMU). On SPG initiative, the Church of England followed up Toronto with the 1965 Lent course *No Small Change* (based on the MRI document), used by over two-thirds of English parishes. Jointly published by the societies and MECCA, this was dispatched from USPG (now blessed, in its two buildings, with the biggest basement in the Church of England). USPG initiative was also behind the 1967 ecumenical Lent course, *The People Next Door*, which greatly stimulated thought and action at the grassroots and marked a significant step forward in inter-Church relations.

It had become clear that some major internal restructuring was needed if the Society was to adapt to the changing face of mission. USPG sent its own Finance Secretary, Frank Chappell, to study modern management principles and adapt them to the Society's purposes. The staff reorganisation took place in 1968, that of committees in 1969, both with astonishing smoothness. The Society's present structures are essentially what emerged then.[5]

There are four Divisions. 'Appointment & Training' is responsible for the College of the Ascension and for home staff appointments as well as selection, training and placement of missionaries overseas. The Overseas Division keeps in touch with missionaries and finds out from overseas Churches their needs for men and women, prayer, and money. Communication with the home Church is the Home Division's task. 'Finance' speaks for itself!

Any communicant of any Church in the Anglican Communion may be elected an Incorporated Member, but USPG does not regard itself as a membership society: 'We look to all baptised Anglicans for support in carrying out the aims of the Society, which are not our aims, but those of the whole Church.'[6] Policy is decided by the Council (President, Vice-Presidents, eighty Incorporated Members, and representatives of dioceses and universities), carried out by the General Committee (Council chairman and two vice-chairmen, ten other Council members, the four Divisional Committee chairmen, and the Society's chief executive, the Secretary).

In 1970 USPG lost a much-loved father-in-God when at the request of the Archbishop of Canterbury Bishop Trapp, chief architect of the United Society, answered a call to Bermuda. USPG now called as its Secretary Ian Shevill, energetic Bishop of North Queensland in Australia.

The new structures worked well, but structures are meaningless apart from the ends they serve. A deeper self-examination had begun: in a world of independent overseas Churches, what was USPG *for*? In 1921 the Society had been charged with mission in six continents: what did this mean in practice—and how to get it across at parish level? Missionary societies must by their very nature be on the frontiers of Christian thought and action, but if they fail to carry their constituencies with them, they will soon cease to exist.

Helping the heathen in foreign parts gave a reassuring sense of superiority, but the old glamorous missionary appeals (splendid money-raisers!) are 'not on' in a Britain whose own National Health Service would collapse without overseas doctors and nurses. Overseas Churches have their own priorities: more than ever before, we need to listen, evaluate requests, and respond appropriately.

> Our task is to forward the preaching of the Gospel. Our aim will always be to encourage overseas Churches to become self-sufficient, so that our help can go into new work. We are not a Society for the Preservation of the Gospel in a Christian Ghetto, but for its Propagation, for making it spread and grow.[7]

But foreign parts now see *us* as a mission field[8] and wonder how *they* can help with the evangelistic task in Britain. When the Anglican Consultative Council (ACC) first met, at Limuru in Kenya in 1971, a majority of the delegates were dark-skinned: the Anglican Communion is no longer a Western thing. The second ACC meeting, in Dublin in 1973, stressed that

> the responsibility for mission in any place belongs *primarily* to the church in that place. However, the universality of the Gospel and the oneness of God's mission mean also that this mission must be shared in each and every place with fellow-Christians from each and every part of the world with their distinctive insights and contributions. If we once acted as though there were only givers who had nothing to receive and receivers who had nothing to give, the oneness of the missionary task must now make us all both givers and receivers.[9]

125

When the Society's seal was designed, we were the Minister on the ship; when the *Centurion* sailed again in 1951-2, it carried overseas missionaries to Britain. For many it is a new experience to stand on the shore in a Posture of Expectation and say 'Come over and help us'. Dublin proposed regional consultations to replace the old haphazard, piecemeal arrangements, the Church in each area inviting those it wants as partners to share in its planning. One of USPG's current tasks must be to help the home Church prepare for our regional consultation, when our sister Churches overseas will help us plan and carry out mission in Britain.

Increasingly, USPG has tried to share with the home Church the thinking of overseas Christians: we .may not always agree with them, but we do need to listen. Its 1968 study course *On the Spot* focused attention on that year's Lambeth Conference and the WCC Assembly at Uppsala.

By this time the theological debate was causing the trumpet to give a very uncertain sound. The traditional view of mission continued to stress evangelism, proclaiming a salvation which includes victory over death: 'If in this life only we have hope in Christ, we are of all men most miserable.'[10] The emphasis was 'vertical', on man's relationship with God.

The 'horizontal' emphasis of the new 'secular theology' saw mission as working for a fully human life in this world, especially by changing social structures seen as impeding this. Political means must be used, even (if all else fails) violence. The mediaeval doctrine of the 'just war' was invoked to support a theory of 'just revolution' not unlike that which tore SPG's American mission field apart in 1776.[11]

Secularisation reached its climax at Uppsala, where the political split between East and West, both industrially developed, gave way to an economic polarity between the 'rich, white North' and the 'poor, coloured South'. This 'Third World', rejecting both capitalism and Marxism (seen as a form of Western liberalism), called for action against injustice. One result was the controversial WCC grants to organisations combating racism ('freedom fighters' or 'terrorists', according to taste). One began to hear of 'black theology'. The battle-cry was 'justice'—a splendid standard for self-examination, but, on the lips of those whose indignation was selective, more suggestive of exchange of roles than of change of heart.

At the opposite extreme in a world-wide polarisation of Christian thinking, the 1970 Frankfurt Declaration saw 'secular theology' as betraying the Gospel through conformity to a world in rebellion against God. USPG's Bishop Shevill was to prove 'both an early spotter, and a setter, of the trend away from a sociological Gospel'.[12]

The controversy split Churches and congregations and the hearts of men, cutting the nerve of evangelism and diverting support to other forms of mission. Many asked if Oxfam and Christian Aid did not minister to human need more effectively, unaware that these excellent organisations rely on missionary societies to staff many of the projects they finance.[13] Some mistakenly linked the missionary societies with the controversial WCC grants. Others, aware of Muslims, Sikhs and Hindus in Britain, wondered about the uniqueness of the Gospel.

Missionary society income dropped sharply while overseas needs continued to grow. Early in 1971 USPG had £348,000 worth of requests for *new* work and only £60,000 available: 100,000 copies of an eight-page tabloid, SPREAD,[14] set out the hard facts and brought a good response, but that year USPG *turned down* £300,000 worth of urgent appeals. In February 1971 the Anglican societies sent a joint letter about the crisis to all English incumbents, parochial church councils and synods, followed up by joint consultations around the dioceses and a serio-comic filmstrip about 'Mr Global Christian', a little round man who knows about the world but after settling into an English parish grows buttons on his ears and on his pockets.

The situation improved, but in 1971 alone the value of the pound dropped nine per cent, and the inflation rate has risen steadily since. USPG's annual income stabilised at around £1.2 million,[15] and no on-going USPG-aided work was abandoned. But even before the energy crisis it was clear that world-wide inflation must accelerate a profound rethinking of the Society's role.

The theological split began to be transcended in 1973. At the Bangkok meeting of the WCC Commission on World Mission and Evangelism, Third World insistence on genuine partnership was summarised by CWME Chairman Emilio Castro: 'We are at the end of a missionary era, and at the beginning of world mission.' But an awareness of different levels of consciousness also emerged, and the 'Christendom' ideal of a homogeneous Christian community began to yield to a more mature fellowship which can tolerate diversity of gifts within the Body of Christ and acknowledge the same Spirit at work in all.

CHAPTER TEN

USPG Today

*A new mission field—New ways of communication
Old ways of renewal—The real revolution
Power and powerlessness—A new style of mission
Voluntary societies?—A ship under sail*

LAMBETH 1958 CALLED South America 'the neglected continent', whereupon the South American Missionary Society
(SAMS) in ten years quadrupled the number of its missionaries.
SPG (which had worked in English-speaking Guyana since 1835
but never in *Latin* America) noted the challenge, but in the light
of other commitments decided against. When Lambeth 1968 said
it again, USPG felt obliged to reconsider the matter. Feeling that
the venture should be ecumenical, it approached the Methodist
Missionary Society (MMS), who were enthusiastic. Exploration
began in 1969, in constant touch with SAMS and the Roman
Catholics as well as with Latin American Anglicans and
Methodists. Early in 1971 a joint USPG/MMS delegation toured
six Latin American countries: 'Down the length of South
America from Colombia to the Argentine, and across the
Christian spectrum from Romans to Pentecostalists, South
America said "Yes" to the idea.'[1]

Thus was born the Anglican-Methodist Project in Latin
America (AMPLA). The opportunities were immense.

> South America is seething with economic revolution.
> Whether the revolution takes creative or destructive courses
> remains undecided. The mission of the Church is to affect
> the revolution for good. The reformation going on in the

Roman Catholic Church is a very deep change for South America—thoroughly biblical, strongly missionary, and resolutely ecumenical. The evangelical Churches, confident of being grasped by the Holy Spirit, are reaching out for wider understanding of God's work in the world.[2]

Buenos Aires was chosen as the base, with invitations from the Anglicans and Methodists there and offers of help from Roman Catholics, Evangelicals and Pentecostalists. USPG and MMS now looked for a team of varied backgrounds,

to learn to be a presence among, and a resource for, the Churches in the continent. It will be, at first at any rate, a 'being' sort of mission, keeping time for prayer, study, reflection, and growth in awareness of the Argentine scene: responding to the missionary situation as a whole, in a continent where the under-twenty-ones are already a majority of the population, where the historic Church has often been locked in with the structures of illiberal governments, where development is galloping (often with no more regard for the poor than has been characteristic of the stagnant past) and where the Pentecostal Churches are growing faster than any other Christian movement in history.[3]

By mid-1974 the team included two English couples and an Argentinian, all Methodists.

Bishop Shevill, aware in his wide travels of the hunger for good Christian material for broadcasting, appointed to the USPG staff an Australian experienced in this work, Robert Browne. USPG's first 'radiotapes' were thirteen simple, direct fifteen-minute talks on 'This Christian Faith' by speakers of the calibre of the Archbishops of Canterbury and York. Sets went to South Africa, Fiji, the USA, Liberia, the Seychelles, Bermuda, Sarawak and Canada; Mozambique translated them into Portuguese. In Britain, parishes began experimenting with these 'Teach Tapes' for house groups and confirmation classes.

A new look was given to USPG's visual aids by Tony Taylor, a professional film-maker. Two 'multi-media' productions (*Towards a New Missionary*, on the meaning of mission as seen at the College of the Ascension, and *Something More Important than*

God? on Latin America) used the latest two- and three-screen techniques to flash contrasting simultaneous images at the viewer (e.g. a cocktail party flanked by dire poverty and street violence). These have proved great discussion-provokers among students and other articulate groups.

In 1973 the Society's Parish Picture Service stopped sending out traditional 'mission pictures' and began sending instead posters designed to make people think.

> A great improvement [said one vicar]. They have a serious theological theme which can be incorporated into a church's worship much more fully than the old descriptive and often trivial pictures.
>
> A positive step away from paternalistic mission attitudes [said another]. I'm sure that the division between 'Home' and 'Foreign' has to go, if only because some aspects of the first are more foreign to some of us than the second.

Some didn't want to think:

> Please concentrate on pictures of the Church at work overseas—a British slum is not relevant to USPG surely.

And one inadvertently asked the $64,000 question:

> Why must our money, raised after great effort, be used to subsidise posters which appear to say that we ought to change our convictions?[4]

Unfortunately some of those 'convictions' *undo* our missionary efforts overseas.

> Missionary societies in the UK must take seriously their inescapable responsibility of effecting a change of heart in the people of their own country towards the hundreds of thousands of citizens from developing countries right in their midst before they go abroad for 'foreign mission',

said the West Indian Acting Principal of Codrington College in 1973.[5] Foreign parts see our post-Christian paganism, our economic selfishness, our disintegrating family and community life, our blindness to human need, our indifference to God and the things of God, and what we are speaks so loudly that they cannot hear what we say. In 1701 their message was 'Come over and help us': today it is 'Physician, heal thyself.'

It is now two years and almost four months since I left my

131

native country in order to teach the Georgian Indians the nature of Christianity; but what have I learnt myself in the meantime; Why (what I the least of all suspected) that I who went to America to convert others was never myself converted to God.[6]

Not long after Wesley wrote that, he *was* converted. He went on to launch the only effective Christian response to Britain's industrial revolution. At its heart was Pietism—rather out of fashion just now, but, as Bray was corresponding with Pietism's founder when he founded SPG, perhaps we should look again. Spener's proposals for renewal of the Church were Bible study in house groups (*collegia pietatis*), lay participation in Church government, practice of Christianity as well as knowledge about it, a sympathetic approach to unbelievers, preaching to implant Christian faith in the inner man so as to transform life, and reform of theological training to give primacy to the devotional life. Not a bad programme, when you come to think of it.

Authentic personal piety, so far from being incompatible with involvement in the world, is the only truly Christian preparation for it. Livingstone's was a secular mission, but Livingstone was no secular missionary. A year before he died (already in great pain) he wrote in his diary:

My Jesus, my King, my life, my All: I again dedicate my whole self to Thee. Accept me, and grant, O gracious Father, that ere this year is gone I may finish my task.

During the Livingstone centenary in 1973, Canon Kingsnorth observed that 'his uncomplicated Victorian piety may be difficult for the post-death-of-God missionary, but he has to win through to something like it if he is to share the Church's mission.'[7]

Primitive Methodism was not unlike modern Pentecostalism (and the somewhat similar African Independent Churches) in its emotional appeal to the rootless, its moral discipline, and its charismatic phenomena such as 'speaking with tongues' and gifts of healing. St Paul's caution is justified,[8] but today's charismatic movement is kindling new fire in countless lives right across the theological spectrum. Immense sub-rational energies are emerging from the 'great deep' over which the Spirit broods.

The Indian subcontinent (where the ghost of Malthus walks)

focuses the world's ecological crisis; southern Africa, its race-relations drama; in Latin America economic and political problems are writ large: irresponsible wealth and desperate poverty, top-heavy bureaucracies, foreign-dominated economies rotten with graft and inflation, violence in daily life.

> This week the cost of basic foods—bread, rice, coffee, sugar —all went up by between 50 and 100%. There was considerable public disturbance and strikes in some cities as a result. Some people were killed by the military.[9]

The Latin American word of hope is *conscientisation*: growth in consciousness, of one's situation and of one's capacity for self-help. People talk of a 'theology of liberation'.

In USPG's 1974 Report, Peter Wyld wrote of 'the romantic simplicities of violence', without which it seems impossible to attract attention in today's world.

> The trouble with violence is not only that it works, but also that men like it: and there . . . is the central problem confronting theology. If the Christians had taken human nature more seriously, we might have more to say now to the warrior instinct of a generation aflame at the injustice in the world, bombing, mining, hijacking, kidnapping—the knight-errants of the late twentieth century, seeking as we did to hallow the violence in themselves through a cause beyond themselves. It ill becomes anyone . . . who has known the simple bliss of war as a young man to look prune-faced at the young men who do it again in their turn and in their way. . . .
> The furnace of aggression . . . is the fire of life itself in immaturity. If your small children *don't* show aggression, start fussing. The problem is not how to douse it but how to mature into handling it. Grudge is as strong a fountain of violence as injustice . . . The Freudian insight into the way we tick is as important as the Marxist one. We must not imagine that every discontent has a rational economic basis, nor that the last demand has been made on love when justice is achieved. The heart of man is not that simple, and the games people play are often designed to maintain rather than to remove discontents.[10]

The Third World has mostly thought of liberation in terms of struggle—against colonialism, racial tyranny, economic or cultural domination. 'We have yet to reckon with the fact that in the deepest biblical sense of that concept the Christian Church is in itself a movement of liberation,' says a leading African Christian.[11] 'It is cruel and sub-christian,' comments John Kingsnorth,

> to suggest that this deeper liberation is not available to a man unless he is liberated politically. There is no biblical, historical or contemporary evidence to suggest that all the world will ever be liberated politically, and those who claim it will, have a very emaciated view of sin. Yet freedom in Christ is available to all men.[12]

The unique salvation offered by Christ does not require changing our circumstances: the liberating truth is that *nothing* can separate us from the love of God.

But to those who crave polarisation, reconciliation must seem subversive. In 1971 Gonville ffrench-Beytagh, then Dean of Johannesburg, was tried and convicted for his undiscriminating Christian charity. When his interrogators defended apartheid by quoting the Levitical prohibition of bestiality,[13] ffrench-Beytagh realised with a shock that

> apartheid went far deeper than an economic and political denial of human rights and dignity. It was an attempt to split off all the 'black', animal part of our nature, with the fears and hatred and sexual drives which we dare not acknowledge even to ourselves, and thrust it into a race whose skin happened to be 'dark'. . . . I had had no idea of the depths of this fear and envy of 'blackness'. . . . I suddenly saw what apartheid was in fact all about. . . .
> My own response to apartheid was equally a 'gut' reaction which was triggered off by my need to hold fast to my integrity as a whole human being against a force which was trying to control and diminish me. God knows, I had enough of 'blackness' in myself, of irrational fears and insecurity and sexual drives. But I can survive only if it is acknowledged and healed and redeemed, not banished to some mental Bantustan.[14]

When one has glimpsed one's own 'blackness', there are two ways to recover one's nerve: a crusade against the darkness 'out there', or a reconciliation which must begin with the alienated 'dark brother' within. 'Agree with thine adversary quickly,' says our Lord: Jacob wrestled with his all night before acknowledging the Living God and receiving his new name; only then could he see the face of God in the face of his brother (instead of his own projected hostility) and accept his brother's forgiveness. The conventional wisdom, Jesus observes, is to love your neighbour and hate your enemy, 'but I say to you, *Love your enemy'*— because God himself loves all equally, just and unjust. That is the real revolution, which makes men whole. Not for nothing is the first of the Messianic signs the opening of the eyes of the blind.

Is this not what 'black' theology is really about? There is more to the Biblical underdog's-eye-view of history than the political aspirations of the oppressed. 'Black' theology involves accepting into articulate consciousness, as redeemed by Christ, the whole 'under side of creation': *black is beautiful!* It involves perceiving the complementarity of opposites, for God who divides light from darkness sees that both are good. It is Adam coming to terms with the ambiguity (good *and* evil) in all creation, and accepting responsibility. 'Freedom to blame is a stage on the way to maturity'—a necessary stage, for without polarisation and conflict there are no defining limits to tell us who we are—but 'maturity itself is freedom to forgive and be forgiven'.[15]

'*Wilt* thou be made whole?' says our Lord to a man who has been making excuses for thirty-eight years. Not everyone wants to be liberated from dependence, but to discover that one *can* stand up and walk is liberation indeed. The revolution in the world is 'the reverberation of the preaching of the Gospel . . . God's teaching of men and nations to stand on their own feet, and work as free men and not as needy children,' said Bishop Neil Russell in 1969, lately returned to Scotland after thirty-four years in East Africa.[16] One cannot help wondering about the spiritual effect of the Church of England's continuing subsidy from the past (the average English diocese is even today only sixty per cent self-supporting): perhaps we need a 'Three-Self' movement in Britain?

Ian Shevill ended his vigorous spell at the helm of USPG in 1973, accepting a call to the see of Newcastle, New South Wales. In his place came Canon James Robertson, a Scot with acute theological perception and wide educational and administrative experience in Zambia and the UK. In the USPG Chapel the Archbishop of Canterbury, blessing Robertson for his work as Secretary, spoke of 'the radical revolutionary remaking of man himself'.

Robertson's arrival happened to coincide with the energy crisis. We talked for years of the changing world, observed Peter Wyld,

> and then suddenly in 1973 it really did. For the first time since the Muslim onslaught on Europe was checked a thousand years ago, the power of the Christian (so to speak) West was held, indeed was held to ransom, in 1973.
>
> The worst thing about the Islamic invasions of the early middle ages was the entrenching of enmity: confrontation between 'us' and 'them', as on the 38th parallel in Korea or the 17th in Vietnam. . . . We never beat the Muslims, and we certainly never taught them the love of Christ . . . . The Christian West simply bypassed the heartlands of Islam and grabbed the east: till 1973, when . . . we suddenly find ourselves again in a world that is not controlled by white men.[17]

'The crazy escalation of standards of living in the West had to come to an end some time,' wrote Bishop Lesslie Newbigin from Madras. 'It is strange that so few of us guessed that this would be the way it would come.'[18]

In the first industrial revolution, Britain had the safety-valve of emigration for malcontents and unemployed; today we can export neither our problems nor the over-production demanded by costly technology, and (though no politician dares whisper it) in a finite world 'economic growth' becomes a euphemism for inflation. 'Salvation will come,' says a Brazilian theologian,

> by extending a poor style of life to the whole of humanity . . . when the world as a whole, especially the wealthy world, the wealthy elements in a given society, understand that we cannot have a society in which all of us share this greedy mood of consuming more and more, but on the contrary when we decide that we have to stop somehow, and that we must learn to consume less.[19]

Adam gets into trouble because he can't say No, when he ought to, to something in itself good. He is also warned that he must earn his keep by the sweat of his own brow: there is no free lunch. One man's cheap labour and raw materials are another man's poverty.

That Western expatriates for so long came as conquerors or affluent benefactors has distorted the role of the expatriate as such. The thing about the stranger in the Bible is his powerlessness. It is as oppressed aliens in Egypt that Israel becomes the People of God (in their Promised Land they become oppressors in their turn). The early Church is by its faith estranged from the pagan world. Expatriation is the spiritual condition of the faithful in every age. And it is the expatriate's mission to disturb (we should be grateful to our brown British neighbours): his alien presence reminds a homogeneous society that its homogeneity is not an absolute. By his foreignness the Christian expatriate also witnesses to the catholicity of the Church—by what he *is*, not by what he does.

'Too many of us have a guilty conscience unless we are actively doing something,' said USPG Council Chairman Archie Hardie in 1973. 'More and more I am convinced that it is the people who *are* rather than the people who *do* who convey the joy of the Gospel to others.'[20] The same year Harry Morton (then MMS General Secretary) said of AMPLA:

> It's going to be a very long haul. . . . We shan't find our way for two or three years. . . . There's bound to be nothing to show for a good bit. It's that sort of job—*being there instead of knowing best*. . . . I feel in my bones that we're on to something: a fundamental break-through in style of mission, even more than in co-operation between Churches.[21]

What might this new style of mission be? No more tidy job-descriptions: that much is clear. Something like the Indian *ashram*, perhaps? Or like what the SSM are doing since moving from Kelham to the new city of Milton Keynes?—turning the Sacred Mission inside out, so that instead of sending chaps out in all directions you're just there—a 'still centre' with a deep, con-templative tap root—and people come to you.

Some other clues came in Bishop Shevill's time through two USPG-supported overseas missionaries to Britain. From the Church of North India came John Sadiq, formerly Bishop of Nagpur, for two years as 'Missionary Bishop of the CNI in the United Kingdom'. Based at the College of the Ascension, Sadiq travelled widely and spoke wisely, especially of a humbler, more Christ-like approach to non-Christians.

> Christianity has not exhausted Christ, nor does it have the monopoly of communicating him. To *see* Christ in other men and *be* Christ-like to other men is the essence of this approach.[22]
>
> We do not really understand what it means to be a missionary until we recognise that what Jesus is doing is not collecting Christians: he is renewing Creation. . . . The essence of mission is the commendation of Christ.[23]

'There's a developing country right on our doorstep,' observed *Network* in 1971, 'and USPG has a missionary at large in it. It is the England of the emerging young, and the man propagating the Gospel is John Erb, Youth Secretary.'[24] This large Canadian priest in the trendy gear came fresh from the Caribbean and turned the image of USPG upside down with all-night vigils in cathedrals, week-end starve-ins, youth festivals, camping trips to Taizé. 'USPG has become synonymous in some quarters with new progressive thinking, but it is difficult for some other supporters to understand what all this is about,' said Erb, in the understatement of 1973. In his first year, 'We talk about programmes, structures, money, but never about Jesus'; two years later, 'We must look for *poor* means to serve.'[25]

In country after country men are being ordained for various forms of 'supplementary' ministry. Bishop Zulu of Zululand prefers to call it 'the self-supporting ministry: it is a full ministry of priesthood.' Sheer economics requires such 'poor means', but in fact

> it is a great step for the future, a return to the Church of apostolic times when all the local leadership was self-employed. . . . Many people in the Church believe as I do that every community (if given the vision and opportunity by Church authority) will throw up its own priest.'[26]

And from SPG's old American mission field comes word that Albany diocese is to try an experiment pioneered in Alaska, whereby one member of a congregation is (after due preparation) ordained solely to celebrate the sacraments, while preaching, leading prayer groups, Bible teaching, youth work, visiting, involvement in social action, counselling are shared by others.

> We're beginning to picture each congregation as a miniature seminary where everybody receives constant training and spiritual empowerment and renewal, and from which nobody ever graduates. Our seminary-trained priests will serve as a roving faculty, equipping lay persons for ministry. . . . Instead of requiring one full-time priest to be good at 20 things, let's help 20 people each develop one ministry skill.[27]

The idea, which is spreading all over the United States, began in 1960 when somebody read former SPG missionary Roland Allen's newly republished *Missionary Methods*.

'A *being* sort of mission, keeping time for prayer, study, reflection, growth in awareness': how to train people for *that*? The present Selly Oak set-up (including the College of the Ascension) is the product of the Secular Sixties: do we perhaps need to think again? In a world of crumbling community and family life, high mobility, and obsession with techniques, where does anyone, lay or ordained, receive the basic spiritual formation the College of the Ascension was founded to provide? Are we taking too much for granted?

USPG has experienced a sharp drop in recruitment; in particular, in mid-1974 no Anglican member of the AMPLA team had been found. *Why*? Do we ask *too little*? Twells of Bloemfontein and Steere of UMCA evoked missionary vocations by stiffening their demands. Some of the Society's finest work has been done through missionary brotherhoods—an idea first suggested by Codrington in 1710. Sheer economics may well stop the sending of married missionaries, at least with families. Should we return to something like the old UMCA terms of service?

At home, both the Friends of USPG and the AMC took shape in response to the needs of the 1950s: do we need different forms of commitment today? Ought we to have a sort of 'Third Order'—open to all Anglicans, not just USPG supporters; perhaps, since mission today must be increasingly ecumenical, to all Christians prepared for that sort of discipleship? USPG, like SPG, enables the mission of others; ought we also, like UMCA and CMD, to be ourselves a mission, in God's one world?

In Bishop Shevill's time, USPG and CMS began exploring together the complementary roles of our two societies. There is now an ongoing working party with a permanent (CMS-appointed) chairman and (USPG-appointed) secretary; and steady progress has been made. Co-operation among all Anglican missionary societies and their involvement in home mission continue to grow.

But do we still need voluntary societies? If so, how ought they to be related to the General Synod's BMU?

Mission is the task of the whole Church, but human nature being what it is, everybody's responsibility is nobody's business. However, the Church has recognised special missionary vocations ever since the Holy Spirit said 'Separate me Barnabus and Saul.' He said it, incidentally, to a Church that was waiting on God with fasting and prayer. At Toronto in 1963, the Bishop of the Sudan, commending from the floor the use of the *QIP*, affirmed that 'prayer is the secret weapon given by the Lord himself, and the people of prayer can hold the balance of power in the world. Men and money are not absolutely necessary to keep the Church alive; *prayer is*.'

Societies are far better than any central board for communication at the grassroots and for dealing with persons; they also have the necessary flexibility to explore new ways of working and to operate outside the official ecclesiastical structures. On the other hand, overseas Churches now prefer to deal with Churches. Ought the General Synod officially to recognise the societies as the way the Church of England in fact works? We must have the confidence of the hierarchy (in the early nineteenth century CMS hadn't), but not be so identified with it as to be indistinguishable (as SPG too often was). The societies themselves decided in 1974 that at each regional consultation overseas a single delegate should represent all societies concerned with that area, and at two of the first five such consultations the societies' representative also officially represented the Church of England as such.

At the time of writing, USPG's future consists more of questions than of answers. And that, under God, is a far better basis for 'being there instead of knowing best' than the old, too simple certainties. Faith is not the same as certainty: its opposite is not doubt but fear. There are things that do not change, and unless we are rooted in them, we are too insecure to risk the openness of real meeting with other minds. The Gospel itself does not change, but its expression must take many forms. 'The totality of truth is not in any one version of words,' says USPG Secretary James Robertson. It is a constant temptation

> to magnify one aspect of the Gospel to the detriment of the whole. When this happens the witness falters and conviction wavers. What we need to be encouraged by is the variety of ways in which gospel-rooted people respond to the world in their living encounters with it.[28]
> USPG needs prophetic insight as well as firm practical policies set by a noble tradition. Both need to be tested in the lives of those whose faith is in the Gospel, whose hope is for the Kingdom and whose charity is rooted in their union with God.[29]

Every institution, it is said, is the lengthened shadow of a man. As you enter USPG House, you are met in the front hall by Thomas Bray, that 'examplary parish priest' who yet

> found time and energy to rouse the Church to great neglected duties, and to design and set in motion societies for their accomplishment, which have carried on his purpose to ends far beyond all that even he foresaw.[30]

Alongside Bray's portrait are William III and a facsimile of his 1701 Charter. On the half-landing opposite hangs the Masasi Crucifix, given in thanksgiving for the work of UMCA from 1857 to 1965. Black theology, carved in ebony, confronts white gentlemen and their words. Both proclaim the incarnate Word and his strange work. It may be that that suffering but triumphant black Man—that poor Man, possessing nothing—speaks more eloquently to our generation.

The ship launched in 1701 is still under sail, now one of a varied fleet going to and fro on God's mission. Is it mere coincidence that what calls USPG House to prayer as the first work of each day is a ship's bell?

Footnotes

FOOTNOTES TO
INTRODUCTION

1 In 1973 there were 525, including wives.
2 Peter Wyld in *What on Earth?*, the USPG 1969 Report, p. 9.
3 'An Outline History of the United Society for the Propagation of the Gospel' in *CMS/USPG Consultation* 8-10 February 1973, (available from either society), p. 11.
4 *The Seeds of Time*, SPG 1963 Report, p. 63.
5 Quoted by Michael Cassidy in 'The Third Way', *International Review of Mission*, January 1974, pp. 16-17. Webster has also long been associated with CMS.
6 *CMS/USPG Consultation*, p. 11.

FOOTNOTES TO
CHAPTER ONE

1 See Max Warren's excellent *The Missionary Movement from Britain in Modern History* (SCM, 1965). The quotation from Carey appears on page 22.
2 SPG *Journal*.
3 Heirs of both the fifteenth-century Hussites of Bohemia and the mediaeval Waldensians of Italy, the Moravian *Unitas Fratrum* was reorganised as a Church under Pietist influence in Germany in 1727 and recognised by the British Parliament in 1749 as 'an ancient episcopal church'.
4 J.S.M. Anderson, *History of the Church of England in Colonies and Foreign Dependencies* (Rivingtons, 1845-56), Vol. 2, p. 611.
5 Bray founded 111 libraries in all, 50 overseas and 61 in England and Wales.
6 W.O.B. Allen & E. McClure, *Two Hundred Years: History of SPCK* (SPCK, 1898).

7 The original Charter may still be seen in the USPG Archives Room. A facsimilie in the front hall shows the alteration made by Royal Assent in 1965 when SPG and UMCA merged into the United Society for the Propagation of the Gospel.

8 H.P. Thompson, *Into All Lands:* The History of the Society for the Propagation of the Gospel in Foreign Parts 1701-1950 (SPCK, 1951), p. 36.

9 The term 'Anglican', which did not in fact come into use until well into the nineteenth century, is used for convenience throughout.

10 *Letter on Quakerism*, presented by Keith in response to SPG's request for information about the religious situation in the colonies.

11 Recorded in the Appendix to the SPG 1706 *Report*.

12 i.e. the daily offices of Morning and Evening Prayer.

13 Frank Klingberg, *Contributions of the SPG to the American Way of Life* (Church Historical Society, Philadelphia, 1943), p. 41.

FOOTNOTES TO
CHAPTER TWO

1 USPG archives.

2 William Andrews, in SPG *Journal*, 12 February 1714.

3 USPG archives.

4 USPG archives.

5 J. McLeod Campbell, *Church History in the Making* (General Synod of the Church of England, 1946), p. 98.

6 Le Jau's 1705 report to SPG, in Appendix to SPG *Journal*.

7 SPG *Journal*, Appendix.

8 R.P. Stacy Waddy, *A Ship Under Sail* (SPG, 1950), p. 26.

9 SPG 1741 Annual Sermon.

10 USPG archives.

11 Pronounced 'Kway-koo'.

FOOTNOTES TO
CHAPTER THREE

1 Letter of 5 April 1759 to the Society.

2 Gardiner Day, *The Biography of a Church* (privately printed, 1951), p. 11.

3 The same year Wesley, his ministers refused ordination by the Church of England, reluctantly ordained two himself.

4 Klingberg, *op. cit.*, p. 37, 42.

FOOTNOTES TO
CHAPTER FOUR

1 Thompson, *op. cit.*, p. 38.

2 *ibid.*, p. 141.

3 SPG 1830 Report.

4 In fact, SPCK was still supporting the 'Danish' mission in South India.

5 John Goodwin, 'An Outline History of the Church Missionary Society', in *CMS/USPG Consultation* of 8-10 February 1973.

6 At first known as the Society for Missions in Africa and the East.

7 An excellent brief statement is contained in the report of the *CMS/USPG Consultations* of 8-10 February 1973.

8 Alan Webster, *Joshua Watson*: The Story of a Layman, 1771-1855 (SPCK, 1954), p. 31.

9 The 'Madras System' (simultaneously promoted by the Nonconformist Joseph Lancaster) was adapted by Dr Arnold of Rugby into the prefect system and is used today in mass literacy campaigns the world over.

10 Christopher Wordsworth (the poet's brother), one of the Hackney Phalanx, later Master of Trinity College, Cambridge.

11 John Inglis (son of Charles), a lifelong friend of Watson: SPG missionary and rector of Halifax, later Bishop of Nova Scotia.

12 J.B. Ellis, *The Diocese of Jamaica* (SPCK, 1913), p. 57.

13 Five years later, his health restored, Pinder became first Principal of Wells Theological College.

14 Thompson, *op. cit.*, p. 173.

15 J. McLeod Campbell, *op. cit.*, pp. 91-92.

16 C.W. LeBas, *Bishop Middleton* (Rivingtons, 1831), Vol. I, p. 192.

17 C.J. Grimes, *Towards an Indian Church* (SPCK, 1946), p. 68.

18 He was also Chaplain to the King, Rector of St Mary-le-Bow and of Loughton, Essex, Archdeacon of Taunton, Prebendary of Wells, and Canon of Lichfield!

19 J. Bateman, *Bishop Daniel Wilson* (Murray, 1860), Vol. II, p. 15.

20 Thompson, *op. cit.*, p. 113. The difficulty in arousing grassroots missionary enthusiasm experienced by Churches which have central mission boards confirms the wisdom of the English pattern of voluntary societies.

21 Available to all Church of England missionary societies, the ABE has in practice been mostly used by SPG/USPG, and its administrative work is done by USPG.

22 The last Royal Letter on behalf of SPG was issued in 1853.

23 Shared with SPCK. He was also rector of Paddington.

24 Son of William and future Bishop of Oxford, one of the most eloquent advocates SPG ever had.

FOOTNOTES TO
CHAPTER FIVE

1 Occupied during the Napoleonic wars and bought from the Dutch in 1814.
2 Lewis & Edwards, *Historical Records of the Church of the Province of South Africa* (SPCK, 1934), p. 13.
3 In Grahamstown, built with a £500 SPG grant refused by Cape Town!
4 Webster, *op. cit.*, p. 132.
5 Renamed, when Dublin and Durham joined, the Universities' Mission to Central Africa.
6 Mary Anderson-Morshead, *History of the Universities' Mission to Central Africa*, 1859-1909 (originally published by UMCA in 1897, revised for the Jubilee, and reissued in 1956 for the Centenary as Vol. I of a three-volume history), p. 5.
7 Anderson-Morshead, *op. cit.*, p. 9.
8 *ibid.*, p. 12.
9 *ibid.*, p. 14.
10 Mackenzie took no part in this, though his party did. All were involved in a later skirmish, helping some Nyasa chiefs recover villagers captured by Yao.
11 Anderson-Morshead, *op. cit.*, p. 25.
12 Within fifty years UMCA's African staff would include 22 clergy and over 300 readers and teachers.
13 Anderson-Morshead, *op. cit.*, p. 47.
14 Mabruki was 'much surprised to find how many English people do not go to church, and asked if they were Christians'. *ibid.*, p. 54.
15 *ibid.*, pp. 53-4.
16 *ibid.*, p. 45.
17 *ibid.*, p. 58.
18 *ibid.*, p. 67.
19 *ibid.*, p. 57. Steere's own wife, at whose urging he had gone to Africa, was never able to join him.
20 This original settlement was at what is now Mkomaindo, about three miles from modern Masasi.
21 Anderson-Morshead, *op. cit.*, p. 90.
22 For three years these two were partly supported by an annual grant of £300 from SPG, which from 1867 to 1882 also provided UMCA with office space, received its funds and kept its accounts.
23 He would later be bishop of Zanzibar (1901-08) and of Northern Rhodesia (1910-14).
24 Anderson-Morshead, *op. cit.*, p. 220.
25 *ibid.*, p. 223
26 *ibid.*, p. 225.
27 *ibid.*, p. 225-6.
28 A model of the *Chauncy Maples* can be seen in USPG House today.

29 Anderson-Morshead, *op. cit.*, p. 185.

30 *ibid.*, p. 172.

31 Thompson, *op. cit.*, p. 199.

32 One suspects, behind this zeal for Royal authority, Evangelical fear of the dominant Tractarianism of the South African Church. SPG experienced similar tensions in India and elsewhere. SPG supported bishops right across the theological spectrum but it did back the right of the Church to control its own life.

33 Just when Darwin's *Origin of Species* (1859) and the liberal theological *Essays and Reviews* (1860) seemed to many to be undermining the very foundations of religion, the Bishop of Natal published some Biblical commentaries reflecting the new 'higher criticism'. Charged with heresy and deposed, Colenso appealed to the Privy Council. The controversy (which produced a tiny schismatic 'Church of England in South Africa') dragged on in Natal for many years.

34 SPG gave £500 for the bishop's stipend and £200 for missionaries.

35 Lewis & Edwards, *op. cit.*, p. 401.

36 With the foundation of the Community of St Michael and All Angels, Bloemfontein Cathedral became in 1874 the first in the Anglican Communion to restore the daily Eucharist.

37 Lewis & Edwards, *op. cit.*, p. 403.

38 Quoted in A.W. Lee, *Charles Johnson of Zululand* (SPG, 1930).

39 With £2,500 a year from SPG. USPG still gives very substantial financial help.

40 SPG 1881 Report.

FOOTNOTES TO
CHAPTER SIX

1 In 1851 SPG had 44 missionaries in India, Ceylon, Burma and Malaya; by 1900 it would have 246, including 64 women.

2 In South India, for a variety of reasons, the Church spread more rapidly and among higher castes.

3 Government officials in India were then required to maintain a studious public neutrality about religion, whatever their private beliefs.

4 *The Story of the Delhi Mission* (SPG, 1917), pp. 2-7.

5 SPG *Journal*, 17 July 1857.

6 *The Story of the Delhi Mission*.

7 His grandfather of the same name had succeeded Josiah Pratt in 1816 to become one of CMS's greatest Secretaries.

8 Which SPG supported with a grant until 1891.

9 A striking feature of nineteenth-century mission is the extent to which it was financed by the very substantial gifts of a relatively few. One donor alone, Miss Angela (later Baroness) Burdett-Coutts, personally endowed three missionary bishoprics: Cape Town and Adelaide in 1847, British Columbia in 1858.

10 McLeod Campbell, *op. cit.*, p. 164. There is, alas, no record of protest by SPG—still too close to the Establishment to prophesy against it.

11 *ibid.*, p. 164.

12 H.H. Montgomery, *Charles John Corfe* (SPG, 1927), p. 43.

13 The term of service was five years at first; today the minimum is three years.

FOOTNOTES TO
CHAPTER SEVEN

1 *Mission Field*, February 1939.

2 'The Ladies' Association for the Promotion of Female Education in India and other Heathen Countries in connection with the Missions of the Society for the Propagation of the Gospel.' In 1894 its title was changed to 'The Women's Missionary Association for the Promotion of Female Education in the Missions of the SPG.' In 1897 it began supporting medical work as well.

3 Thompson observes (*op. cit.*, p. 231) that the JCMAs in 1891 were 'in part a move by insurgent youth against the conservatism of the autocratic old Secretary.'

4 It also made the Archbishop of Canterbury President *ex officio*, and all English and Welsh diocesan bishops Vice-Presidents.

5 Lady Montgomery, *Bishop Montgomery* (SPG, 1933), p. 49.

6 This continued until 1927, then turned into *The Church Overseas* (1928-34) and *The East and West Review* (1935-62), the last two being published jointly with CMS.

7 An enormous amount of work in the Society headquarters is done by a dedicated group of regular voluntary helpers.

8 SPG 1911 Report.

9 As Archbishop Tait's chaplain, he had been on the SPG committee whose report led to the 1882 Supplementary Charter.

10 A.G. Blood, *History of the UMCA*, Vol. II, p. 43.

11 *ibid.*, p. 14.

12 Quoted by John Peart-Binns in 'A Turbulent Bishop' in the *Church Times*, 10 September 1971.

13 1904 SPG Report, p. 132.

14 SSM typescript of *c*. 1930, quoted by George Every in his introductory Memoir to Kelly's *The Gospel of God* (SCM, 1959), pp. 27-8.

15 Reprinted by the World Dominion Press in 1960.

16 Then covering only the southern part of the present diocese (the northern part being in UMCA territory). SPG gave £500 endowment and £1,000 for the first five years.

17 The SACRM followed the railway from Mafeking to Bulawayo and, briefly, into Northern Rhodesia. The Central Africa section has in recent years become the Railway Mission of Rhodesia and Botswana.

18 Blood, *op. cit.*, Vol. II, p. 215.
19 Six weeks each year in the bishop's own house, with an annual three-week refresher course for priests.
20 1941 SPG Report.
21 Blood, *op. cit.*, Vol. III, p. 13.
22 Thompson, *op. cit.*, p. 634.
23 Thompson, *op. cit.*, p. 539.
24 A principle not, alas, observed by Roman Catholics nor by the many sectarian and 'one-man' missions.
25 The evangelisation of its own contemporaries is of course the duty of *every* Christian generation.
26 Published by SPCK.
27 *College of the Ascension Jubilee Newsletter, 1973*, p. 2.
28 Blood, *op. cit.*, Vol. III, p. 17.
29 Quoted by Michael Ramsey in his lucid account of Anglican theology, *From Gore to Temple* (Longmans, 1960), p. 159.
30 *ibid.*, p. 160.

FOOTNOTES TO
CHAPTER EIGHT

1 Canon Noel Strong in Miss Lea's obituary in the *Church Times*, 3 September 1971.
2 Blood, *op. cit.*, Vol. III, p. 112.
3 Refitted with a diesel engine in 1967, the '*C.M.*' plies Lake Malawi today as a ferry.
4 At the Lausanne Faith and Order Conference in 1927; quoted in Carol Graham, *Azariah of Dornakal* (SCM, 1946), p. 110.
5 A comparable ecumenical dilemma in South India soon after 1706, it will be recalled, had led to SPCK's taking over work which SPG could not assist.
6 *Living is Belonging*, SPG 1959 Report, p. 36.
7 John V. Taylor in the March 1973 *CMS-Newsletter*.
8 By SPG. Son of the Society's former Secretary, Stacy Waddy (long an SPG missionary in India) was then Warden of the College of the Ascension.
9 *Forward from Fifty-one*, SPG 1952 Report, p. 26.
10 In 1949 an exhibition of African art from the art school at Cyrene in Southern Rhodesia (founded by SPG ten years before) had toured England. The publications referred to are *Life of Christ by Chinese Artists* (1938), *Son of Man: African and Indian Art* (n.d.), and *Indian Artist's Life of Christ* (1949).
11 *Forward from Fifty-one*, p. 28.
12 *ibid.*, p. 8, 10.
13 *ibid.*, p. 31.

14 *ibid.*, p. 21.

15 *Continued Steadfast*, SPG 1954 Report, p. 106.

16 The JCMA, which had never really recovered from the First World War, had dissolved itself in 1931, entrusting the *QIP* to SPG.

17 In 1955 it was easier for the West Indian bishops to confer in London than in the Caribbean.

18 In 1969 a decrease in their own numbers compelled them reluctantly to withdraw.

19 *Seeds of Time*, SPG 1953 Report, p. 75.

20 The Minister for Bantu Affairs, quoted in *No Time to Waver*, SPG 1955 Report, p. 31.

21 At least, since 1776!

22 *The Restless Ones*, SPG 1957-8 Report, p. 37.

23 It was at this time that 'stewardship' caught on—imported from SPG's original American mission field.

24 Blood, *op. cit.*, Vol. III, p. 386.

25 *ibid.*, p. 395.

26 *ibid.*, p. 397.

27 The 1974 change of regime in Portugal puts a huge new question-mark over the future of the whole of southern Africa.

28 Osmund Victor, *The Salient of Africa* (SPG, 1945), p. 67.

29 In its parish council constitution, sent to USPG in 1971 and quoted by the writer in *Starting From Here*, the USPG 1972 Report, p. 111.

30 One third of the nearly £33,000 USPG sent to Malawi in 1974 was for medical work.

31 *This World and the Next*, USPG 1974 Report, p. 99.

32 Report of the Toronto Anglican Congress, 1963, p. 1 (summary by the Editor, E.R. Fairweather, in his introduction).

33 *ibid.*, p. 16.

34 *ibid.*, p. 13.

FOOTNOTES TO
CHAPTER NINE

1 *Supplement to the History of the UMCA, 1957-65* (USPG, 1965), p. 8.

2 In 1974 it works mainly in fifteen of the twenty-seven provinces of the Anglican Communion: Australia, Burma, Central Africa, England, the Indian Ocean, Ireland, Japan, South Africa, South East Asia, the South Pacific, Tanzania, Wales, West Africa and the West Indies, and in the Churches of North and South India.

3 John Kingsnorth soon after the merger, quoted by Peter Wyld in *What On Earth?*, the USPG 1969 Report, p. 8.

4 The idea of training some for mission in Britain was not new: the old College of the Ascension had trained many a parish worker for the home Church.

5 A detailed outline of USPG structures and operations is included in the report of the *CMS/USPG Consultations*, 8-10 February 1973.

6 Graham Leonard, then Bishop of Willesden and Chairman of the USPG Council, in *CMS/USPG Consultations*, p. 12.

7 George Braund, (USPG Travelling Missioner 1968-73, now Overseas Secretary), in *Globespell*, USPG's tabloid review of 1973, p. 3.

8 No new thing, actually. About the time SPG missionaries were being thrown out of America for political reasons, a Seneca Indian named Red Jacket remarked of missionaries generally, 'Why do they send them among the Indians? The white people are surely bad enough to need the labour of everyone who can make them better.'

9 Dublin report, *Partners in Mission* (SPCK, 1973), p. 53.

10 1 Cor. 15.19.

11 This whole debate was already in the making when SPG was born: revulsion from the horrors let loose by religious zeal in seventeenth-century politics led to Pietism's withdrawal from politics and the humanitarian Enlightenment's rejection of religious zeal.

12 *Globespell*, p. 3.

13 USPG alone received £175,000 from Inter-Church Aid's 'Freedom from Hunger' campaign, for agricultural projects in Borneo, Malawi, India and Pakistan.

14 This tabloid format was in 1972 adopted for *Network*, whose circulation has risen to around 30,000.

15 Almost exactly the same as the General Synod's entire budget for 1973.

FOOTNOTES TO
CHAPTER TEN

1 SPREAD, September 1971, p. 6.

2 *ibid.*

3 *Network*, November 1972.

4 These and other reactions were printed in *Network*, September 1973.

5 Kortright Davis, at the 1973 AMC conference at High Leigh. Davis is also Associate Director of Christian Action for Development in the Caribbean.

6 John Wesley, *Journal* (Everyman edition), Vol. I, p. 75.

7 *Network*, May 1973.

8 1 Cor. 14.

9 John and Hilary Hopkin of the AMPLA team, while doing language study in Bolivia. *Network*, July 1974.

10 *This World and the Next*, pp. 43-4.

11 Burgess Carr, General Secretary of the All Africa Council of Churches, quoted by John Kingsnorth in *Network*, June 1974. Christians writing to SPG from Maoist China in 1951 *did* recognise this.

12 Kingsnorth, *loc. cit.*

13 Leviticus 12.23.

14 Gonville ffrench-Beytagh, in his autobiography *Encountering Darkness* (Collins, 1973), pp. 7-8.

15 Peter Wyld, *loc. cit.*

16 *What On Earth?*, USPG 1969 Report, p. 1.

17 *This World and the Next*, p. 6.

18 *ibid.*, p. 8.

19 Aharon Sapsesian, interviewed in connection with *Somerhing More Important than God?*

20 *Network*, September 1973.

21 *Globespell*, p. 2 (emphasis mine).

22 *Network*, December 1972.

23 *Network*, January 1974.

24 Jim Nagel in *Network*, December 1971.

25 *Network*, December 1973.

26 *This World and the Next*, p. 30.

27 Bishop William Gordon of Alaska, in *The Albany Churchman*, January 1974,

28 *Network*, April 1974.

29 Preface to *This World and the Next*.

30 Thompson, *op. cit.*, p. 43.

INDEX